Student Handbook to Sociology

History and Theory

Volume I

Student Handbook to Sociology

History and Theory

Volume I

SHANNON K. CARTER

LILLIAN O'CONNELL

ANNE BUBRISKI-McKENZIE

Liz Grauerholz
General Editor

Facts On File
An Infobase Learning Company

Student Handbook to Sociology: History and Theory
Copyright © 2012 Shannon K. Carter, Lillian O'Connell, Anne Bubriski-McKenzie

Facts On File, Inc.
An Imprint of Infobase Learning
132 West 31st Street
New York NY 10001

Library of Congress Cataloging-in-Publication Data

Student handbook to sociology / Liz Grauerholz, general editor.
   v. cm.
  Includes bibliographical references and index.
  Contents: v. 1. History and theory—v. 2. Research methods—v. 3. Social structure—v. 4. Socialization—v. 5. Stratification and inequality—v. 6. Deviance and crime—v. 7. Social change.
  ISBN 978-0-8160-8314-5 (alk. paper)—ISBN 978-0-8160-8315-2 (v. 1 : alk. paper)—ISBN 978-0-8160-8316-9 (v. 2 : alk. paper)—ISBN 978-0-8160-8317-6 (v. 3 : alk. paper)—ISBN 978-0-8160-8319-0 (v. 4 : alk. paper)—ISBN 978-0-8160-8320-6 (v. 5 : alk. paper)—ISBN 978-0-8160-8321-3 (v. 6 : alk. paper)—ISBN 978-0-8160-8322-0 (v. 7 : alk. paper)
  1. Sociology. I. Grauerholz, Elizabeth, 1958–
  HM585.S796 2012
  301—dc23   2011025983

Facts On File books are available at special discounts when purchased in bulk quantities for businesses, associations, institutions, or sales promotions. Please call our Special Sales Department at (212) 967-8800 or (800) 322-8755.

You can find Facts On File on the World Wide Web at
http://www.infobaselearning.com

Text design and composition by Erika K. Arroyo
Cover printed by Yurchak Printing, Landisville, Pa.
Book printed and bound by Yurchak Printing, Landisville, Pa.
Date Printed: April 2012
Printed in the United States of America

10 9 8 7 6 5 4 3 2 1

This book is printed on acid-free paper.

CONTENTS

FOREWORD   vii

INTRODUCTION   1

1 PURPOSE OF SOCIAL THEORY   3

2 HISTORY OF SOCIOLOGY   11

3 EARLY CLASSICAL SOCIAL THEORISTS   19

4 LATER CLASSICAL SOCIAL THEORISTS   39

5 THREE MAJOR PARADIGMS   57

6 SOCIAL LIFE AND THE REALM OF IDEAS   73

7 POSTSTRUCTURALIST AND POSTMODERN THEORIES   89

8 FEMINIST THEORIES   105

9 THEORIES OF EMANCIPATION   119

10 THEORY AND THE REAL WORLD   135

GLOSSARY   143

BIBLIOGRAPHY   153

INDEX   155

FOREWORD

You might wonder why we begin this *Student Handbook of Sociology* series with a volume on social theory rather than a dozen or more cool topics that sociologists study. The reason is that social theory is at the heart of all that sociologists do. Why sociologists study what they study, how they go about studying these particular topics, what is considered to be sociological and what is not—all comes back to social theory. Sociological inquiries—whether they focus on child abuse, employee-employer relations, self-concept, or social revolutions—all emerge from sociological perspectives, and these perspectives are the off-spring of social theories. Hence, if you want to understand sociology, you must appreciate the theoretical frameworks that guide sociological inquiries. As you delve into the other volumes in this series, you will see how these same theories are used to frame and understand a wide range of sociological issues.

This volume outlines the dominant sociological perspectives and provides a historical context for understanding how these perspectives emerged. It also introduces perspectives that have received less attention from mainstream sociology but are important in understanding society as a whole, especially the lives of those people who have been marginalized through much of history. What all of these theories have in common is a concern with what the authors of this volume call the "big question": What is society? And whether they espouse the classical or contemporary perspective, all social theorists seek to understand how society works. What varies is which aspect of society or social life they seek to bring into focus.

All theories offer important insights, but there have been and continue to be debates about which perspectives are most valuable. Some perspectives have fallen into and out of favor, enhanced or diminished by greater social forces operating at any given time. Sociological theories reflect all social phenomena:

When, why, and how they emerge cannot be separated from prevalent cultural and historical forces.

As the authors of this volume explain, sociology emerged as a discipline because massive social change taking place in society gave rise to new concerns and issues that individuals sought to understand and solve. Sociological theories that explained or interpreted social realities have emerged and changed over time, revealing the history of sociology as a discipline.

Thus, the purpose of this volume is not only to provide insight into the history of sociology and important sociological theories but also to show the value of the sociological perspective. This perspective, as you will learn as you read through the *Handbook*, encourages us to step outside of our own narrow world and see how our lives are profoundly shaped by other forces. As you'll see, when and why theories emerge, and when and why sociology as a discipline emerged, can be traced directly to historical and cultural contexts that gave rise to the ideas that shaped both the theories and the discipline. As you begin to understand that sociology and sociological theories are social phenomena that are subject to change and are influenced and redefined by social and historical shifts rather than being static and unchanging, sociology comes to life, encouraging you to interact with these ideas in exciting ways.

—Liz Grauerholz, University of Central Florida

INTRODUCTION

Sociology emerged as a discipline in the 19th century as academics in Europe and the United States envisioned a new field of study that would focus on human societies. Through their writings, they defined the methodological and theoretical approaches sociologists could use in their academic work. As sociology developed, vast social changes—particularly in the realms of technology, communications, and civil rights—produced a need for new understandings of the social world.

This volume traces the history of sociology and the development of sociological theory over time. Chapter 1 defines sociological theory and provides a few examples of different ways sociologists view the social world. Chapter 2 provides an overview of the history of sociology and sociological thought. In this chapter we describe the social conditions under which sociology as an academic discipline was established, such as the Enlightenment, industrialization, and urbanization. We examine the relationship between these broad social changes and the development of a discipline that sought to explain them. Chapter 2 also provides a brief description of each theory and the social context in which it was created.

Chapters 3 and 4 summarize the work of the major classical theorists, who wrote during the 19th and early 20th centuries. These theorists created sociology and worked to define its research methods and theoretical approaches. They also conducted the first sociological investigations, providing insights that are still valid today. As you will see in these chapters, early sociologists were not all in agreement over what society is and how it should be studied. Instead, they laid a foundation for different ways of viewing the social world that together make up a sociological perspective.

Chapter 5 begins the discussion on contemporary theory, which consists of theories developed primarily after World War II. The chapter explains the three major theoretical paradigms in sociology: structural functionalism, conflict theory, and symbolic interactionism. In Chapter 6 we explain phenomenology, ethnomethodology, and critical theory, which extend the symbolic interactionist and conflict paradigms discussed in the previous chapter.

In Chapter 7 we move into even more contemporary times, summarizing theories that were developed in the 1970s, 1980s, and 1990s. We begin with the work of Michel Foucault, a French theorist who examined language as a mechanism of power in society. We then move into postmodern theory, which argues that technological developments have brought about significant social changes. Finally we summarize the work of synthesists, sociologists who bring together and integrate conflicting ideas from previous theories.

Chapters 8 and 9 focus on emancipatory theories, which analyze systems of social domination in an attempt to bring freedom to oppressed groups. Chapter 8 examines feminist theory, which has a long historical development and has been studied through the prism of a variety of theoretical approaches. Chapter 9 examines theories of race and ethnicity, postcolonialism, queer theory, theories of nonhuman animals, and environmental theories.

Chapter 10 concludes the volume with an examination of the ways sociological theories are used in society. In this chapter, we discuss the relationship between sociological theory and research, political activism, and public policy.

CHAPTER 1

THE PURPOSE OF SOCIAL THEORY

This book provides an overview of the history of sociology and development of sociological theories over time. All ideas are produced within a particular sociohistorical context, so it is important to understand when and under what conditions different sociological perspectives were created. This chapter explains the purpose of social theory and its role in sociology.

WHAT IS SOCIAL THEORY?

A **theory** is a set of ideas about how something works. It provides a framework, or lens, for understanding a certain topic or issue. A theory is different from a fact in that a fact can be proven true or false; a theory cannot be proven to be true or untrue. Instead, a theory can be used to provide valuable insights about a particular topic. In this sense, theory is similar to philosophy.

Because a theory cannot be proven true or false, it is considered valid if it is generally accepted among experts of a field. If experts believe a theory is useful for understanding topics they study, that theory will be accepted as valid. If a theory is not accepted by experts as being useful for understanding topics of interest, then that theory will not be considered valid. Within each field, not all experts will agree on the usefulness of individual theories. Some experts will favor some theories while others will favor other theories. As long as a significant number of experts consider a theory useful, it will continue to be used in the discipline. Theories also fall in and out of favor, often in response to social and political changes that make some theories more relevant than others in certain sociohistorical contexts.

A **social theory** is a set of ideas about how society works. It provides a framework, or lens, for understanding a social topic or social issue. Many social theories are used in sociology, and not all sociologists agree on which social theories are the best. As long as some sociologists advocate and use a particular theory, that theory continues to be included in the discipline.

One way to understand social theories is to think of them as different lenses, like sets of eyeglasses. A certain pair of glasses will enable us to see the world a certain way. For example, glasses with orange-tinted lenses will show an orange-hued world. Things that are yellow, orange, and red might appear brighter and more noticeable with orange glasses than without. On the other hand, things that are blue and purple might appear darker and more difficult to see. Through green glasses, things that are green and blue might appear brighter; things that are red and yellow might be harder to see. We can think of social theory the same way—as a set of lenses that make certain things stand out with more clarity than others.

If we look at society through the lens of one theory, certain parts will be easier and other parts more difficult to see. This is because different theories focus on different parts of society. If we look at society through the lens of a different theory, the parts that were difficult to see through the first theory might be easier to see with the second theory. At the same time, what was easy to see through the lens of the first theory might be more difficult to see through the lens of the second theory.

The view of society and the individual through the lens of structural functionalism exemplifies this point. The theory of **structural functionalism** focuses on broad social structures and institutions in society. **Social structures** are parts of society that are separate from individuals within society, but that guide their actions in patterned ways. The social structure itself is not a tangible thing we can see. What we can see, however, is patterned and predictable behaviors that show the impact of social structure on individuals.

Social institutions (also referred to as **institutions**) are broad social structures that have a recognized purpose in society, structures such as education, economics, politics, healthcare, and family. In sociology we refer to such institutions in a broad sense. For example the "education institution" refers to all schools, colleges, universities, teachers, administrators, textbooks, buildings, and so on that collectively make up all "education" in a society. So, when we look at society through the lens of structural functionalism we see society as a complex set of structures and institutions. We see broad, overarching patterns in society. For example, we can see that the educational institution serves as a kind of "babysitter" so parents (workers) can be involved in the economic institution. The education system then takes on the task of teaching children

The Sociological Imagination

Sociology seeks to understand how society shapes and is shaped by individuals, or the relationship between social forces and individual actors. Sociologist C. Wright Mills called the ability to view individual circumstances in terms of the social forces that contribute to them the *sociological imagination*. The sociological imagination requires the ability to view personal troubles—issues or hardships experienced by individuals—as public issues, or broader social problems that originate in the structure of society. For example, when hearing about someone who is unemployed, many people assume the person is unemployed as a result of personal failures or characteristics, such as laziness, poor educational choices, or lack of work ethic. Conversely, the sociological imagination requires individuals to look beyond personal characteristics and view the circumstance in terms of the broader social structure. A sociological imagination reveals that unemployment can be caused by economic downturn, corporate downsizing, and outsourcing of jobs to less industrialized nations. Indeed, there are fewer jobs than there are workers in U.S. society, so unemployment is a built-in feature of the social structure. Mills believed the ability to recognize the connection between social forces and individuals varies from person to person, as the sociological imagination exists at the intersection of history, biography, and social structure. Since every person has a unique biography, the sociological imagination of all people will vary somewhat, even if individuals share history or exist within the same social structures. Nevertheless, individuals can use their sociological imaginations in everyday life to help understand the world around them.

skills they need to be productive members of society. Because structural functionalism is focused on these broad patterns in society, it does not focus on individuals. To study interactions among individuals in everyday life, we need a different theory.

We can see here how one theory provides a lens that makes certain parts of society more noticeable. By emphasizing one part of society, that theory deemphasizes other parts, making them more difficult to see. This is why we have many different theories in sociology. As students of a whole body of knowledge, we want to see and be able to understand all parts of society. But each theory allows us to see only a particular part. This does not mean the theory is flawed or wrong; it simply means the theory is focused on one aspect of society and not all. The obvious corollary to this is that different theories emphasize different things and are not necessarily contradictory.

In his book *Critical Social Theory*, Craig Calhoun argued there are many different ways to look at a single topic. Calhoun suggested that it is not possible to ask (and answer) all really interesting questions about a topic with just one theory. Each way of looking highlights a different part of the topic. When we are able to look at a topic through the lenses of all sociological theories, then we have a complete understanding of the topic from a sociological perspective. As a result, there are many theories in the field of sociology.

A comparison of structural functionalism to symbolic interactionism illustrates how each theory makes some parts of society easier and other parts more difficult to see. **Symbolic interactionism** views society not as a system of social structures and institutions, but as individuals interacting with each other in everyday life. This theory emphasizes individuals in society and their actions and interactions. Because symbolic interactionism focuses on individuals, it does not emphasize social structures and institutions. So, if we look at society or a social topic through the lens of symbolic interactionism, we will focus on the individuals in society rather than on the broad social structures and institutions. If we look at society or a social topic through the lens of structural functionalism, we will focus on broad structures and institutions and not on individuals. Like different colored glasses, each theory makes some parts of society easier and other parts more difficult to see. As sociologists, we are interested in the answers all the theories provide. Together, the different theories make up the sociological way of looking at the world.

THE BIG QUESTIONS

Social theory deals with what we might call the "big questions" in sociology. These are questions about things that are fundamental to the discipline. Some of the big questions in sociology are:

- What is society?
- What is sociology?
- How should sociology be conducted?

The answers to these questions are not as clear-cut as they might seem. Take for instance the question, "What is society?" We could probably give a straightforward definition of this concept and be done. Many sociologists define **society** as a system of patterned interactions that encompasses a social structure, social institutions, and social interactions in everyday life. This gives us a definition that we can use to communicate, but it fails to answer some of the bigger philosophical questions about what society is and where it comes from.

How we define society depends on which theory we use. Remember that structural functionalism focuses on broad social structures and institutions. From a structural functionalist perspective, this is what society is. In other words, structural functionalists view society as a system made up of broad social structures and institutions. Structural functionalists view society as a separate construct from the individuals in the society. Emile Durkheim, an early sociologist and founder of functionalist theory, insisted that society should be thought of as an entity or force that exists outside of individuals. Durkheim argued that if society were just made up of the people in the society, then we would have no need for sociology; instead, we could just study psychology because the society would reflect the psychological status of the people. Durkheim also asserted that although we cannot see society because it does not have a physical, tangible presence, we can see its effects. That is, we can see the ways society shapes us. From this perspective, society is a set of broad social structures and social institutions.

The theory of symbolic interactionism defines society very differently. Symbolic interactionists believe society is made up of individuals. Whereas structural functionalists argue society exists "out there," separate from the individuals in the society, symbolic interactionists argue society is "right here," in the everyday interactions between individuals. According to symbolic inter-

Symbols such as the American flag are so important that the U.S. government chose to place one on the moon when Apollo 11 landed in 1969.

actionists, individuals communicate in everyday life through the exchange of shared symbols. A **symbol** is something that represents something else. A flag, Star of David, peace sign, and smile are all examples of symbols. They are symbols because the objects or gestures have no intrinsic meaning themselves but are given meaning by members of society. Members of society collectively agree upon the meanings they give these symbols, and they use the symbols to communicate with one another. Symbolic interactionists point out that **language** is a system of symbols that facilitates communication among people in society. According to symbolic interactionists, individuals work together to create society through the exchange of shared symbols and language. From this perspective, society is a product of interactions among individuals in the society.

It is clear that symbolic interactionists and structural functionalists view society differently. In other words, these two theories provide different answers to the question "What is society?" Each theory provides a distinct set of ideas about how things work and what things are. Other theories would disagree with both views, proposing different definitions of society. In this sense, theory is very much like philosophy. A social theory provides a philosophical orientation for looking at society.

Another big question social theorists seek to answer is "What is sociology?" This question was particularly important to early social theorists who created sociology as a discipline of study. In creating this new discipline, early theorists needed to define the parameters of the field. In other words, they had to decide what exactly sociologists would study and what they would not study. They had to decide whether sociology should try to be scientific and concrete like the natural sciences or whether it should be more in the realm of ideas like philosophy. Not surprisingly, different social theorists came up with different answers.

Auguste Comte is credited for coining the term "sociology." Comte believed sociology should be a science, which means sociologists should use the ideas and methods scientists use to study the natural world and apply them to society. Comte also believed sociology should be a **positive science**, an approach that seeks to uncover verifiable laws of the social and physical world. Comte posited that sociology should seek to discover laws that explain how societies work and that sociology should be used to promote positive social change. Emile Durkheim also believed sociology should be a science. He developed ideas about how sociologists could study society by using the same principles as natural scientists. Durkheim suggested sociologists should identify **social facts**, things that could be observed in all similar societies. According to Durkheim, sociologists should consider social facts as things. In the study of a particular social fact, sociologists should look for **antecedent social facts**, social causes of the social fact being studied. After identifying the causes of a particular social fact (the antecedent social facts), sociologists should examine its consequences. By using the ideas and principles of science, Durkheim argued, sociologists could study society in an objective and unbiased manner. Durkheim also demonstrated how sociologists could study social phenomena using **quantitative research methods**, which rely on numbers and statistics. Because Durkheim advocated sociological methods that were objective and unbiased, he viewed it as acceptable for sociologists to advocate social change based on their research findings.

Max Weber had a different answer to the question "What is sociology?" Weber believed science, and its search for only those phenomena that can lead to generalization, was limiting for sociology. He argued that cases different from the generality should also be of interest. Weber was not advocating that sociologists study individual people who do things differently from the rest of society, but that we should study the particular phenomenon that occurs differently in one or a few societies from what occurs in other societies. Weber used this approach in his study of capitalism. In his book *The Protestant Ethic and the Spirit of Capitalism*, Weber compared the economic systems of different societies. He analyzed the ways one economic system—rational capitalism—developed in many European countries and in the United States but not in other countries, such as China. In this analysis, the economic system of rational capitalism is the individual case that is compared to other economic systems.

Although Weber argued that science is not the best way to study society, he believed sociologists should be value free in their research and teaching. Weber advocated **value-free sociology** in which sociologists set their own values and opinions aside and approach research topics from a neutral position. Weber argued that if sociologists are too invested in their research topics they might be tempted to manipulate results to support their own values. To make sure this does not happen, Weber suggested sociologists should simply seek to uncover facts, or explain *what is*. Then, ordinary people and politicians in a society should use the information created by sociologists to determine *what should be*. With this approach, sociologists can conduct research in a neutral manner without having to rely on (or adhere to) strict scientific methodology.

It is clear that Comte, Durkheim, and Weber all had different ideas about what sociology should be. This is part of what social theory is all about. Because these theorists were writing during the very early years of the emerging discipline of sociology, it was important for them to define exactly what they thought the discipline should accomplish and how it should meet these goals. Once the discipline was established and courses and degrees were offered at universities, it became less important for the next generation of sociologists to define the parameters of sociology or explain specifically what they thought sociologists should focus on. Nevertheless, the debates on how sociology should be conducted and the best way to perform social research continue today.

Further Reading

Calhoun, Craig. *Critical Social Theory*. Malden, Mass.: Blackwell Publishers, 1995.

Cuff, E.C., W.W. Sharrock, and D.W. Francis. *Perspectives in Sociology,* 5th ed. London: Routledge, 2006.

Reynolds, Paul Davidson. *A Primer in Theory Construction*. Boston: Pearson, 2007.

Schneider, Mark A. *The Theory Primer: A Sociological Guide*. Lanham, Md.: Rowman & Littlefield, 2006.

Turner, Jonathan H. *The Structure of Sociological Theory,* 7th ed. Belmont, Calif: Wadsworth, 2003.

CHAPTER 2

HISTORY OF SOCIOLOGY

There is evidence of sociological thinking throughout human history, with individuals taking interest in understanding their social conditions. Sociological scholarship, including lectures and publications, date back to the 1300s and are found not only in Western societies but others as well, including Africa, Asia, and the Middle East. Despite this earlier work, sociology did not begin to emerge as a distinct academic discipline until the 18th century, when scholars in Europe began to create systematic research methods that allowed them to expand and apply these theories.

THE RISE OF SOCIOLOGY AS AN ACADEMIC DISCIPLINE
A set of significant social changes that took place in Western Europe and the United States during the 18th and 19th centuries contributed to the development of sociology as a distinct discipline. This time period was characterized by a fundamental shift in the dominant mode of thought referred to as "the Enlightenment," the Industrial Revolution, and the rise of capitalism.

The **Enlightenment** refers to a shift in the dominant mode of thought from an emphasis on religion and theology to an emphasis on reason, rationality, and science. **Rationality** is defined as the use of careful calculation to determine the most efficient or effective way of completing a task. Enlightenment thinking valued precise calculation and configuration of facts, often relying on scientific methods to distinguish what was factually true from what was not. The Enlightenment facilitated the emergence and growth of academic sociology because intellectuals increasingly relied on science for developing an understanding of the world. This mode of thought naturally led to an interest in scientific reasoning and empirical study of the social world. The predominant idea was that such an understanding could promote positive social changes.

The new emphasis on reason, rationality, and science occurred in conjunction with the **Industrial Revolution**, the period of transformation from agriculture-based to industrial-based society. This transformation was characterized by the growth of factory production where goods were mass produced with the use of advanced machinery. Individuals shifted from making a living through farming and agriculture to finding employment in factories. This shift facilitated **urbanization**—the growth of cities—as individuals and families left their farms to move into cities where factory jobs were available. The Industrial Revolution coincided with the rise of modern **capitalism**, an economic system based on a free market and accumulation of wealth. Mass production of goods made it possible for greater wealth accumulation, as factory owners could oversee production of thousands of goods rather than just the few an individual could make alone. Goods produced in factories were property of factory owners, who could sell mass quantities of goods to accumulate wealth. Accumulated wealth could be invested in another factory, where the cycle could continue. In this way, the Industrial Revolution and the capitalist economic system were mutually complimentary. The Industrial Revolution, urbanization, and the rise of capitalism contributed to the growth of sociology because some intellectuals were increasingly concerned about the impact of these vast social changes on society. Some theorists used sociology as a way to understand these changes whereas others viewed sociology as a vehicle to direct the course of social change.

Early European scholars such as Claude Henri de Saint-Simon (1760–1825) and Alexis de Tocqueville (1805–1859) engaged in sociological theorizing about society. However, it is Auguste Comte (1798–1857) who first coined the term "sociology" and advocated the creation of a distinct academic discipline to analyze society. Comte envisioned sociology as a "positive science," mirroring the natural sciences. Other early theorists, such as Emile Durkheim (1858–1917) and Max Weber (1864–1920) helped define the specific content and methods for the discipline. Durkheim and Weber, along with Karl Marx (1818–1883), Herbert Spencer (1820–1903), and Georg Simmel (1858–1918) used the approaches they created to understand various components of society, such as economics, work, politics, and religion.

There were also a number of women and minorities who contributed to the development of sociology, including European classical theorists Harriet Martineau (1802–1876) and Marianne Weber (1870–1954), American classical theorists Charlotte Perkins Gilman (1860–1935) and Jane Addams (1860–1935),

Changes that resulted from the Industrial Revolution spurred interest in understanding society. *(Wikipedia)*

African American theorist W.E.B. Du Bois (1868–1963), and African American female theorists Anna Julia Cooper (1858–1964) and Ida B. Wells-Barnett (1862–1931). As a result of the sexist and racist structure of Western societies and academia, these theorists' work was largely ignored by white European men who dominated the discipline. Only in the past few decades have efforts been made to revisit the work of these female and minority classical theorists and incorporate it into mainstream sociology.

Much sociological work of female and minority classical theorists focused on the same topics examined by white men, including economics, politics, and religion. Women and minorities, particularly Harriett Martineau and W.E.B.

The Shift into Modernity

Sociology is a product of the time and place in which it was created. Sociology was created at the beginning of the *Modern Era*, a time period characterized by the rise of industrialization, urbanization, and capitalism. These broad social changes occurred in conjunction with a change in the dominant mode of thinking known as the *Enlightenment*, which emphasized reason, rationality, and science. The Modern Era in Western Europe was preceded by the *Feudal Era*. Social order in the Feudal Era was based on *divine right*, the belief that kings and queens had a direct connection to God. People obeyed the rule of the royal family because they believed orders represented God's will. The shift into modernity facilitated the rise of sociology because people began to seek scientific and other nonreligious explanations for social phenomena.

Du Bois, also worked to define the content and research methods of sociology. Some female and minority theorists are distinct from white male theorists in their emphasis on gender and race in analyses of broader institutions, such as economics and religion, and in analyses of issues that might be considered distinct to women and African Americans, such as the home, family and reproduction, and slavery and lynching.

SOCIOLOGY IN THE 20TH CENTURY

By the beginning of the 20th century, a number of sociology departments could be found throughout the United States and Western Europe. Different theories were beginning to emerge, some that stood in opposition to each other. The three most well-known theoretical perspectives are structural functionalism, conflict theory and symbolic interactionism.

Structural functionalism is based on the earlier work of Emile Durkheim and elaborated upon by Talcott Parsons (1902–1979), Robert Merton (1910–2003), Kingsley Davis (1908–1997) and Wilbert Moore (1914–1987). Parsons, an American sociologist at Harvard, envisioned society as a cohesive social system with various parts working together to maintain harmony. This theory gained popularity in the United States during the post–World War II era, which was characterized by a *spirit of consensus*, a sense of cohesion and agreement among society's members.

Conflict theory is based on the earlier works of Karl Marx and Max Weber and elaborated upon by a variety of scholars, including C. Wright Mills (1916–1962), Ralf Dahrendorf (1929–2009), Randall Collins (1941–), and Immanuel Wallerstein (1930–), to name a few. Conflict theorists view society as a set of unequal groups in conflict over power, resources, and values. Conflict theory became prominent in the United States during the Civil Rights era, when group conflict was particularly apparent.

Symbolic interactionism originated at the University of Chicago, commonly referred to as the **Chicago School**. Social philosophers such as William James (1842–1910), Charles Horton Cooley (1864–1929), and George Herbert Mead (1863–1931) laid a philosophical foundation for symbolic interactionism that was developed into a social theory by Herbert Blumer (1900–1987) during the 1960s and 1970s. Symbolic interactionism is largely a response to structural functionalism, arguing that society is not a broad, abstract set of overarching structures and institutions, but rather is made up of individuals interacting in everyday life. Symbolic interactionists posit that individuals interact by exchanging symbols. Through the process of socialization, individuals learn how others around them interpret different symbols, including language, which prepares them to interact with others. Through this collective social action, social institutions and structures are created by individuals interacting in everyday life.

Two theories that are similar to, yet distinct from, symbolic interactionism are phenomenology and ethnomethodology. **Phenomenology** was developed by Alfred Schutz (1899–1959) and is based on the philosophical work of Edmund Husserl. Phenomenology argues individuals maintain different perceptions of the world, and therefore sociology should seek to understand the subjective realities held by individuals. Such an understanding can only be obtained through **qualitative research methods**, a research approach that seeks to obtain in-depth data that focuses on meanings and interpretations that guide social life. **Ethnomethodology** was created by Harold Garfinkel (1917–2011) in the 1970s. Ethnomethodology views the social world as emerging through actions and interactions of individuals. Unlike symbolic interactionism, which views society as relatively stable, ethnomethodology argues that society and social structures are continually being constructed and reconstructed through individuals' social actions.

Critical theory also gained popularity during the 1960s and 1970s. Critical theory originated during the 1930s and 1940s at the Institute for Social Research at the University of Frankfurt, commonly known as the **Frankfurt School**. Some key critical theorists are Max Horkheimer (1895–1973), Theodor Adorno (1903–1969), Walter Benjamin (1892–1940), Antonio Gramsci (1891–1937), and Jurgen Habermas (1929–). Critical theory draws on the works of Marx and Weber to provide a critique of domination in society and discover methods of emancipation. Critical theory analyzes the role of what counts as "knowledge" in a society in perpetuating social inequality. In its critique of knowledge, critical theory is skeptical of the role of science in the production of knowledge, including sociological knowledge.

Michel Foucault *(AP Photo/Alexis Duclos)*

The relationship between knowledge and power continued to be at the center of analysis in the emergence of poststructuralism in the 1970s and 1980s. **Poststructuralism** was developed out of structuralism, a key theory in **sociolinguistics**, an academic discipline that analyzes the role of language in societies, which was formulated in the 1950s and 1960s by theorists such as Ferdinand de Saussure (1857–1913), Claude Levi-Strauss (1908–2009), Jacques Lacan (1901–1981), Roland Barthes (1915–1980), and Louis Althusser (1918–1990). **Structuralism** emphasizes the ways in which language structures human thoughts by providing rules about how ideas can be put together. Structuralists are different from structural functionalists in that structuralists focus primarily on language while structural functionalists focus on society more broadly. They are similar in that each school views its substance areas as existing separate from yet exerting influence over individuals. Poststructuralism, developed by Michel Foucault (1926–1984), Jacques Derrida (1930–2004), Gilles Deleuze (1925–1995), and Julia Kristeva (1941–), draws upon structuralist ideas of language as separate from and shaping the ideas of individuals, and introduces the concept of power and domination into this scheme. According to poststructuralists, domination occurs through limitations on the thoughts individuals are able to think within language. According to Foucault, this domination is not necessarily for the purpose of one group exerting power over another, but to maintain social order, which serves the interests of the state. Foucault argued that state exertion of power over individuals' thoughts through language is an efficient method of controlling a population, one which appears more humane than physical coercion.

Postmodern theory arose in the 1980s and 1990s from the work of theorists such as Jean-Francois Lyotard (1924–1998), Jean Baudrillard (1929–2007), and Fredric Jameson (1934–). Postmodern theorists posit that Western societies are transitioning beyond the modern era into a postmodern era. Jean Lyotard described the **postmodern condition**, as a condition characterized by the expansion of a global market; decline in production of material goods, which transforms the basis of work and economics; and an ideology that questions the validity of science. A key component of the postmodern condition is the **information revolution**, or a transformation from industrial to information-based economy where information increasingly becomes a commodity that is bought and sold. Baudrillard extended these observations, arguing that media representations have increasing power in postmodern society, blurring the boundary between reality and simulation.

The next major trend in sociological theory, occurring during the 1980s and 1990s, was for theorists to revisit previous theories and attempt to create a synthesis that blends old ideas together and mediates disagreements. Two sociologists who engaged in this synthesis are Anthony Giddens (1938–) and Pierre Bourdieu (1930–2002). Giddens created the theory of structuration, which blends symbolic interactionism and structural functionalism. He suggested a two-way relationship exists between structure and individual action. Based on the impact of structure, individuals act in a way that reproduces the very structure that impacted their behavior. Bourdieu brings together subjective and objective knowledge, arguing that individuals' actions are shaped by their location in the social structure, which reproduces that location. In this way, social inequality is reproduced through a combination of structure and individual action. For example, individuals raised in some middle and upper-class households where proper English is spoken are raised to speak proper English, which helps them succeed in school and employment, which helps them maintain their privileged class status. Thus, by engaging in actions they were taught by their location in the social structure, individuals act in ways that reproduce their place in the structure.

Another recent development in sociological theory is **emancipatory sociology**, a theory created for the purpose of eliminating domination. Although emancipatory themes are woven throughout many different sociological theories, from the classical works of Marx, Gilman, Cooper, and Du Bois to conflict and critical theorists to synthesis, many of these earlier theories were either discarded by mainstream sociologists due to the race and gender of their proponents or were created by individuals in positions of power. During the 1990s and 2000s, emancipatory sociology was and continues to be taken seriously in most areas of sociology. In addition, the newer version of emancipatory theorizing has been created by individuals who are members of subordinate groups. Emancipatory theorizing includes feminist theory, theories of race and ethnicity, queer theory, postcolonialism, and theories of nonhuman animals and the environment.

SUMMARY

Sociology began to emerge as a discipline in the early 19th century as important changes in Western societies gave way to new ideas and questions about the social world. Throughout the history of sociology, new ideas about what society is and how it should be studied have been created, theories that coincide with the social concerns of the time periods in which the ideas are produced. At the same time, earlier theories remain relevant and continue to shape the ways sociologists approach their subject matter. Although we expect new theories to emerge throughout the 21st century, these theories will be impacted by the ideas of earlier theorists, who will continue to shape the development of sociology.

Further Reading

Cuff, E.C., W.W. Sharrock, and D.W. Francis. *Perspectives in Sociology,* 5th ed. London: Routledge, 2006.

Ritzer, George. *Sociological Theory,* 8th ed. New York: McGraw-Hill, 2011.

Turner, Jonathan H. *The Structure of Sociological Theory,* 7th ed. Belmont, Calif.: Wadsworth, 2003.

CHAPTER 3

EARLY CLASSICAL
SOCIAL THEORISTS

Several criteria must be met if one is to be considered a classical social theorist. First, the theorist must have published during the early development of sociology, the 1800s and early 1900s. Second, the theorist must have developed a theory that can be applied to a broad range of sociological topics. Third, the theorist's work must be considered relevant by experts in the discipline. In this chapter, we cover the works of early classical theorists Auguste Comte, Harriett Martineau, Karl Marx, and Emile Durkheim.

AUGUSTE COMTE
Auguste Comte (1798–1857) is often credited as the founder of sociology. He is given this title because he created the term "sociology" and outlined a vision for the discipline. Comte preferred the term "social physics" to "sociology" because he thought sociology should be similar to physics, except applied to the social world instead of the natural world. However, Comte discovered Belgian statistician Adolphe Quetelet was using the term "social physics" to describe a study of society that was different from Comte's vision, so he reluctantly began to use the term "sociology" instead. Although Comte was the first to use the term "sociology" and define its subject matter, there were others doing similar work at the time that informed Comte's ideas. This group included Charles Montesquieu, Jacques Turgot, Jean Condorcet, and Claude-Henri de Saint-Simon.

Comte's Vision of Sociology

Comte believed sociology should be modeled after the natural sciences. He believed sociology would be the supreme science (the "queen science" as he called it) because he saw it as the most complex science. Comte envisioned sociology as a "positive science of society." **Positivism** is an approach that seeks to uncover verifiable laws of the social and physical world. Thus, Comte believed sociology should seek to discover laws, or abstract principles, that explain how societies work. Just as Newton discovered the law of gravity that governs the physical world, Comte believed sociologists should discover laws that govern the social world. In Comte's vision, sociologists would search for laws that govern both the organization of societies and changes in societies over time. Sociologists would not be concerned with the causes of the laws but instead would focus on identifying and describing the laws themselves. In seeking to uncover the laws of the social world, sociology would be most like physics, in that both would search for the smallest number of laws to explain the greatest number of cases.

Comte believed sociologists should use both empirical observations and theory to uncover social laws. Something is **empirical** if it can be verified

Auguste Comte, 1798–1857

Auguste Comte was born on January 19, 1798, into a middle-class family in Montpelier, France. Comte was a bright student and after graduating from high school he attended Ecole Polytechnique, a prestigious technical school in France. He did not receive a college degree because a disagreement between the school and the French government caused the school to close temporarily while Comte was a student. In 1817 Comte became a secretary for philosopher Claude Henri de Saint-Simon. The two worked and wrote together for several years until they had a falling out in 1824. Comte married in 1825, but his marriage was wrought with problems. Comte was very intelligent, had a photographic memory, and had high self-esteem with regard to his intellect, yet he had a difficult personality, was arrogant, and suffered from mental problems in his later years, which eventually cost him his friends, his marriage, and the respect of important academics of his time. Comte never held a formal professorial position at any college or university, but he was a teaching assistant and admissions examiner at Ecole Polytechnique for several years. He wrote many books and articles and gave several lectures. Comte died in 1857. Although he was not highly regarded among French intellectuals during his lifetime, Comte's work impacted many influential thinkers in England and the importance of his work was recognized after his death.

through the senses (sight, sound, touch, taste, and smell). **Empiricism** in sociology means that knowledge is gained through empirical research, a set of procedures from which the findings can be verified. In other words, in sociology, we would say we have empirical evidence of something if we have concrete evidence through research that the thing is true. This is different from theory, where we use philosophical ideas to conceptualize how something works. In Comte's view, sociology needed to be an empirical science, where concrete evidence of laws could be observed in society. However, Comte also believed empirical research was useless without theory. He believed empirical research and theory needed to be used together to uncover the laws of society. This way, theory would be verified through empirical observation and empirical observations would be explained through theory.

Comte also advocated a relationship between theory and practice. That is, he believed sociology should be used for the practical purpose of creating positive social change. Before sociology could be used to promote social change, it had to become established as a science and uncover the basic laws of society. Comte believed that once this was accomplished, sociology could be used to direct the course of human history.

Sociological Research Methods

In advocating the use of empirical research in sociology, Comte outlined four research methods sociologists could use to gain knowledge about the social world. The first is *observation*, where the researcher sees evidence of a social phenomenon in the concrete social world. Comte suggested observation should be guided by theory because observations alone were not useful for understanding how societies work.

The second research method is *experimentation*. Comte understood that experiments worked better in some of the other sciences than sociology because social phenomena cannot easily be manipulated or changed. Moreover, using experiments to study some sociological topics would be unethical. For example, we cannot create a war between two nations to study its effects on a society. However, Comte suggested that natural experiments occur in societies when an extraordinary event occurs without instigation from researchers, such as a war or tsunami, and that sociologists can study how societies organize themselves in response to such an event. Just as biologists can learn about the normal functioning of the human body when illness occurs, Comte believed sociologists could learn about the normal functioning of society when a pathological event occurs.

The third research method Comte outlined is *comparison*. Comparison is simply comparing, looking at similarities and differences between one group and another. In Comte's vision, sociologists could compare human societies to nonhuman animals or different human societies to each other.

Comte's fourth research method is *historical research,* a method in which the sociologist compares a current society to its own past. Comte believed historical research would be the "chief scientific device," or most important research method, used by sociologists because it would give them a better understanding of how societies change over time.

Social Statics and Social Dynamics

Comte believed sociology could be divided into two parts: social statics and social dynamics. **Social statics** studies the parts of society and their relationships to each other and the larger social system. Comte's use of social statics focused on ways societies were organized, how social order was maintained, and the broader social structure. Comte viewed society as a whole social system. He believed no part of society could be studied as an independent unit because each part functioned as part of the whole. Sociologists could study each part of society, but each part had to be studied in terms of how it relates to the whole. This vision of society as a system made of parts that work together is what theorists later called *functionalism.*

Comte did not see the individual as the basic unit of society because he believed the individual responds as much to biological needs as to social needs. In Comte's study of social statics, he determined that the *family* was the most basic unit of society. Comte believed other social units, such as tribes, groups, and eventually societies, evolved from the family. In studying social statics, he was interested in discovering the parts of society that helped create *social cohesion,* bonds among a society's members. He believed *religion* was important for moral regulation and facilitating relationships among people, *language* facilitated relationships by allowing communication, and *division of labor* made people in a society dependent on each other. In his analysis of these different aspects of society, Comte emphasized how each relates to the larger whole.

Social dynamics is the study of social change and examines patterns in how societies change over time. Comte believed all societies move through the same stages in their development but that the rate of change may differ from one society to the next. In his study of social dynamics, Comte created the **law of the three stages**, the idea that all societies move through the same three stages in their development: theological, metaphysical, and positivistic. In the *theological stage,* religious ideas—ideas that focus on a supernatural entity—dominate the society. Social bonds are created through religion, with the priest as the social leader. In the *metaphysical stage,* ideas move away from the supernatural but still explain things in a mystical kind of way, or a way that cannot be verified empirically. These ideas are developed and taught by philosophers. Social bonds are created through control by the state, law, and military. Comte believed the metaphysical stage was a bridge between the theological stage and the *positivistic stage* in which ideas are based on science and empiricism. These ideas are developed and taught by scientists. Social bonds are created through mutual interdependence, and the basic operations of society are coordinated by the state.

Comte believed ideas shaped the structure of society and that ideas, or the dominant way of thinking in a society, impact all the different parts of the society, including its political, economic, and educational systems. Comte also believed the course of social evolution was additive, so that new ideas are added to old ideas as a society progresses. He posited that the transition from one stage to the next was not smooth but that the ideas of the different stages conflicted with each other, so the transition from one stage to the next entailed a period of instability and conflict. Comte was convinced that in the positivistic stage (and according to Comte, society was entering this stage at the time he was writing) scientific understanding of society would be possible through his vision of sociology. Consequently, the laws of society discovered by sociologists could be used to create positive social change.

HARRIET MARTINEAU

Harriet Martineau (1802–1876) is sometimes referred to as the "founding mother of sociology" because she was the first scholar to conduct sociological research. Although she did not use the term "sociology" in most of her writing, her work envisioned the development of a discipline that would systematically study society. She referred to this discipline as a "science of society" and a "science of morals." Martineau's work focused on describing the procedures for sociological investigation and then carrying out a systematic investigation using the procedures she described.

Martineau's Vision of Sociology

Martineau viewed the sociologist as a public educator, one who writes not only for an academic audience but a general audience. Indeed, much of her work was written for a general audience. This approach is apparent even in her books on research methods, where she referred to the sociological researcher as a "traveler" or "observer." Martineau envisioned ordinary citizens using sociological research methods to make informed political and personal choices based on scientific understandings of social life.

Like Comte, Martineau believed sociology should be a systematic science of society, based on empirical research. (As previously noted, something that can be verified through the senses is empirical, and empiricism occurs when knowledge is gained through empirical research, a set of procedures through which findings can be verified.) Martineau also believed sociology should be a *critical* science. She proposed that the goal of sociology is not just to observe and report information about societies but also to evaluate them. In particular, Martineau

Harriet Martineau, 1802–1876

Harriet Martineau was born on June 12, 1802, in Norwich, England, into a liberal Unitarian family that lived a comfortable lifestyle supported by a family-owned textile business. Martineau was the sixth of eight children in the family. Although girls were typically afforded fewer educational opportunities during the time, Martineau was provided a good education, just like her brothers, due to the family's liberal Unitarian beliefs, and she was a very good student. Martineau became deaf during early adolescence, but she did not allow this disability to inhibit her work. She began writing articles about the unequal status of women in 1820 for *The Repository*, a Unitarian journal. During the mid-1820s, her family's business began to suffer as a result of a general economic downturn in society. Her father died in 1826 and the business failed in 1829. During this time, Martineau became engaged to marry, but the engagement ended when her fiancé became mentally unstable. Because Martineau was single and deaf, it was decided that she would continue to live with her mother and work to try to support her. She chose to write for a living and wrote a series of novels that aimed to teach the general public about economic theory. Martineau published more than 1,500 newspaper columns and 70 volumes of literature, ranging from academic work and novels to poetry and children's books. Martineau also edited Comte's *Positive Philosophy* and translated it into English. Comte liked Martineau's edited version so much he commissioned a translation back into French, and the translation replaced his original version. Martineau was also a social activist who traveled to different regions of Europe and spoke about equality and women's rights. She died at home on June 27, 1876.

believed sociology should oppose **domination,** a condition in which individuals or groups are denied freedom and autonomy as a result of the will of others. In circumstances of domination, individuals are unable to pursue happiness and act according to their own morals. Instead, they are forced to submit to the will of those who have power over them. According to Martineau, domination can exist in interactions among individuals, where one individual may deny another individual freedom and autonomy. Broader societal practices can also limit individual and group autonomy. Martineau believed that one of the goals of a science of society was to promote social justice, thereby opposing domination.

Martineau believed sociology should evaluate the extent to which a society promotes human happiness, arguing that sociologists could make this evaluation by analyzing the morals and manners of a society. Martineau considered **morals** to be collective ideas about appropriate or inappropriate social behaviors. She viewed **manners** as patterns of actions and interactions within a society. In today's terminology, we might use the word "values" to represent what

Martineau meant by "morals" and "manners" as being the *norms*, or rules, that guide actions in a society. Put another way, "morals" represents the way people think and "manners" represents what they do. According to Martineau, the morals and manners of a society are interconnected. The morals of a society might shape the manners, or they might contradict them. The sociologist's role is to investigate the relationship between morals and manners in a society.

As interpreted by Martineau, the well-being of a society depends on the consistency between the society's morals and manners. When a society professes a set of beliefs but acts in a way that contradicts those beliefs, an **anomaly** exists because morals and manners are not consistent with each other. Once the anomaly is identified, the sociologist's role is to determine the consequences of that anomaly.

Sociological Research Methods

Martineau created a qualitative, interpretive approach to collecting and analyzing sociological data. As explained above, qualitative research seeks to obtain in-depth data that focuses on meanings and interpretations that guide social life. Qualitative research often relies on fewer *participants* (that is, individuals who take part in the study as research subjects) than quantitative research, and the goal of the research is to gain in-depth understanding of participants' experiences and viewpoints. Martineau used **interpretive sociology**, which focuses on uncovering what things mean to people and how they interpret different aspects of social life. Martineau's methodology required the sociological researcher (who could be anyone interested in learning about a society) to visit the society being studied and observe the way of life.

Martineau argued that sociologists must approach a society in a certain way to accurately understand it. First, the researcher must be *impartial*, not invested in any particular outcome. To accomplish impartiality, the researcher must approach the society in a neutral manner and evaluate it on its own terms rather than through the lens of the researcher's own society. Second, the researcher must be *critical* of the society being observed. According to Martineau, the sociologist should be a moral being who engages in a critical assessment of the society. In order to be both impartial and critical, the sociologist must rely upon objective criteria (such as written documents) to evaluate the society. Above all, the sociologist must evaluate the society based on its own morals and not on those of another society.

By insisting that sociologists evaluate each society based on its own moral guidelines, Martineau introduced the concept later known as cultural relativism. **Cultural relativism** is the idea that societies should be observed and evaluated through the lens of their own culture rather than the lens of another culture. Martineau suggested impartiality and critical assessment can be achieved by measuring the extent to which the society promotes human happiness. Human happiness is promoted by societies through social justice, or the absence of domination. Martineau also suggested researchers must be *sympathetic* to understand what things mean to the people in the society that is being studied.

According to Martineau, sociological research should focus on studying *things* and *discourses of persons*. She suggested the collective beliefs and values of a society are embedded in a society's *things*—cultural objects such as music, architecture, institutions, and documents. Although Martineau wrote that sociological researchers should talk with members of the society they are studying, she cautioned that the people researchers came into contact with might not be representative of the society, and therefore the information gathered from talking with individuals might be biased. In connection with this, Martineau believed things in a society would better represent the society as a whole. She believed sociological research should focus on things that exist or occur in all societies, such as food, clothing, and shelter; health and illness; reproduction and death; and how order is maintained. She posited that *discourse*—the ways people talk with one another—could be studied as a thing. In the study of discourse, Martineau believed the common style of interacting in a society—whether people were friendly, sincere, serious, and so on—was more revealing than the meanings of the words used.

Based on Martineau's view that sociology should provide a critical evaluation of societies, she created three criteria for evaluating domination in a society. First, sociologists should investigate the condition of the least powerful groups in a society. Second, they should consider the society's morals in terms of its own views of power and authority. Third, they should evaluate the society's progress in providing freedom from domination.

Martineau's Critique of the United States

Martineau used the methods she created to study the United States and published her findings in a three-volume work titled *Society in America*. In this work, she compared the morals in U.S. society to its manners. Martineau used written documents to determine the morals in U.S. society, especially the Declaration of Independence. She identified the morals of equality ("all men are created equal") and democracy, a government that represents the people it governs. By observing manners (or actions) in U.S. society, she identified four anomalies, specifically manners that contradicted the morals. The anomalies she identified are slavery, unequal status of women, fear of public opinion, and pursuit of wealth.

Martineau argued that slavery contradicted the moral of equality. She believed the consequence of this anomaly was the disruption of happiness and morality for all groups involved, from the slaves themselves, to slave-owning families, to merchants who bought and sold products made from slave labor.

One way slavery inhibited happiness was through its disruption of the family. Under slavery, sexual relations between white male slave owners and their black female slaves were common. Martineau argued that this exploitation of black women's sexuality had a negative impact on black and white men and women, thereby disrupting family stability for both groups. Slavery was an anomaly because it contradicted the morals of U.S. society that purported to promote freedom and equality; it also interfered with individuals' pursuits of happiness.

Martineau suggested that women's unequal status with men also contradicted the morals of equality. She argued that Christianity does not prescribe unequal status to men and women, so the unequal status in U.S. society also contradicted the morals set forth by Christianity. Martineau compared women's status in U.S. society to slavery, suggesting the two were similar in that justice was denied to one group based solely on the will of another group. The domination of women by men encouraged exaggerated gender roles, in which men became stronger, more aggressive, and dominating, and women became weaker, more submissive, and more dependent. She argued that women's unequal status caused their intellect to be confined, both by lack of educational opportunities and because they were discouraged from pursuing science and philosophy. The absence of educational opportunities not only confined women's intellect, but also had negative effects on women's health and economic status. In addition, because women were barred from intellectual and economic pursuits, their only option for a socially acceptable lifestyle was marriage.

The third anomaly Martineau identified was subservience to public opinion. The morals of U.S. society supported democracy, a government based on free speech that represents and is run by the people. However, Martineau observed that individuals in U.S. society feared speaking out against what they believed was "public opinion." Individuals associated public opinion with the majority, and since a democracy is run by the majority, they wanted to consider themselves part of that group. Consequently, individuals were unwilling to speak out if their ideas were inconsistent with what they believed was public opinion. This fear of public opinion inhibited social justice because politicians and the general public did not speak out against other anomalies, such as slavery and women's unequal status.

Finally, Martineau identified the pursuit of wealth as an anomaly in U.S. society. According to its morals, the United States was a republic in which each individual had equal representation. However, in the manners of U.S. society, individuals pursued the accumulation of wealth. One consequence of the pursuit of wealth was that those who obtained more wealth were granted more power, which contradicted the notion of equal representation. A second consequence was that the pursuit of wealth provided little time for leisure and relaxation. Without time to relax, individuals had little time to reflect on their morals.

This lack of time for reflection inhibited individuals' abilities to act in accord with their morals, which in turn contributed to the deterioration of morals in U.S. society. From these collective observations, Martineau concluded that U.S. society was unable to fulfill its promises to its people.

KARL MARX

Karl Marx (1818–1883) viewed human history as the progression toward freedom. Marx's theory of progression is based on philosopher G.W.F. Hegel's idea of the *dialectic*, which suggests the progression of society is the development of ideas. Hegel believed ideas would continue to develop until humans discovered absolute truth. Once humans discovered truth, our purpose would be fulfilled and history would be complete. Hegel's **dialectic mode of logic** is the idea that societies progress through conflict. In his explanation of the dialectic he posited the following: One social group presents an idea, or *thesis*. Another group presents an opposing idea, called an *anti-thesis*. Through conflict, the two groups eventually merge their ideas into a new, better understanding, called a *synthesis*. According to Hegel, the resulting synthesis becomes a new thesis, and the cycle continues until humans reach absolute truth. Once truth is discovered, humans are free and history is complete.

Marx agreed with Hegel's concept of the dialectic, but he believed that societies progress as a result of people's relations in the concrete, material world rather than the realm of ideas. Marx's view of the development of society is referred to as dialectical materialism. **Dialectical materialism** refers to a process of conflict in which one economic system is in place (equivalent to a *thesis*), a group of individuals in this economic system is oppressed, and the oppressed group would benefit from a new economic system (*anti-thesis*). The two groups engage in conflict until a new economic system emerges (*synthesis*). The synthesis then becomes the new thesis, and the cycle continues until absolute political and economic freedom is reached. At this point, humans are fulfilled, and history is complete. Once history is complete, humans do not stop living, but societies stop changing because they have reached their end state, which is complete freedom.

Capitalism

Marx viewed capitalism as one of several economic systems in the progression toward absolute freedom. *Capitalism* is an economic system based on a free market and the accumulation of wealth. In capitalism, the means of production are privately owned and operated. **Means of production** refers to land, buildings, machines, and materials used to produce goods, such as a factory and its contents. Marx observed that the very structure of the capitalist system leads to power disparities, as one group owns factories while another group works in them. This was even more apparent in Marx's time when factories

Karl Marx, 1818–1883

Karl Marx was born on May 5, 1818, in Trier, Prussia, to middle-class parents. His parents were both Jewish but converted to Lutheranism, partly to avoid discrimination and help further his father's career as a lawyer. At age 23, Marx earned his doctorate in philosophy from the University of Berlin. After graduating, he took a job writing for a radical newspaper, which was later shut down by the government because of its radical political leanings. In 1843 Marx married Jenny van Wesphalen. The two eventually had seven children, though only three survived to adulthood due to the family's poverty. After they married, the couple moved from Prussian Germany to Paris, hoping to enjoy the more liberal atmosphere France offered. There Marx met Friedrich Engels, who became a close friend and regular collaborator. Engels was critical of the life conditions of the working class, sentiments that influenced much of Marx's work. Marx did not remain in Paris very long; his writings had profoundly upset the Prussian government, which formally requested the French government to expel him from France. The request was honored; Marx was forced to leave France in 1845, and moved to Brussels, Belgium. The expulsion from France did not temper his radicalism, and in 1848 he and Engels published *The Communist Manifesto*, which details the goals and beliefs of communism. A year later, Marx moved to London, where he began devoting himself to in-depth research on the capitalist system. Altogether, Marx published over 20 books. During his time in London, Marx lived in abject poverty and suffered from personal illness. His wife died in 1881, and Marx himself died two years later on March 14, 1883.

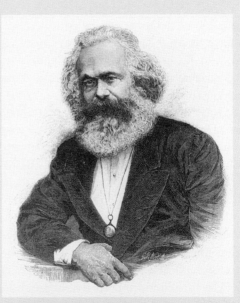

Karl Marx is seen as one of the founders of modern political economic thought.

were owned by a small number of individuals and the majority of the population was made up of workers. Factory owners were wealthy, and workers lived in poverty.

Marx argued that the starting point of capitalism is the circulation of commodities. A **commodity** is a product of labor (such as a television, an orange, or a pair of shoes) that is given value. One form of commodity circulation is the **C-M-C exchange** in which a commodity (C) is exchanged for money (M) that is used to purchase a different commodity (C). For example, a person might grow oranges, a commodity (C), and sell them to get money (M). That money is used to purchase shoes, another commodity (C). Marx, however, argued that it is not the exchange of commodities that is the real thrust of capitalism. Instead, capitalism requires an **M-C-M exchange**, in which money (M) is invested in a commodity (C) for the purpose of making more money (M). For example, a capitalist may spend money (M) to purchase an orange grove, a commodity (C), but this purchase is made solely with the intention of selling oranges to make more money (M). This money (M) may then be invested in a lemon grove (C), and the lemons are sold to make even more money (M). In this sense, money (M) is invested in a commodity (C), which is used to make more money (M). Marx defined money that is put into circulation only to obtain more money **capital**.

The M-C-M exchange can also be considered a *cycle of production* whereas the C-M-C exchange can be considered a *cycle of consumption*. It is important to note that the M-C-M exchange can exist only if the C-M-C exchange exists. Without buyers for goods, production would halt; without production, there would be no goods to consume. Hence, the cycles of production and consumption are interdependent.

Marx argued that the important difference between the two cycles is that in the C-M-C cycle money is spent once and for all whereas in the M-C-M cycle money is only temporarily advanced with the goal of gaining more money. Consequently, capitalists (who use the M-C-M cycle) are concerned with the **exchange value** of goods, the amount of money a good can be sold for. Consumers (who use the C-M-C cycle) are concerned with the **use value**, or practical application of the good. For example, the use value of a house is that it provides shelter whereas its exchange value is how much it sells for on the real estate market. Individuals involved in the C-M-C (consumption) cycle would purchase a house for its use value (shelter) whereas individuals involved in the M-C-M (production) cycle would purchase a house for its exchange value (how much money they can make from it). According to Marx, the defining feature of capitalism is the M-C-M exchange, or the transformation of money into more money. For capitalists, this cycle is never complete, because the objective of capitalism is to continue acquiring more and more money.

Capitalism and Alienation

Marx believed capitalism distorts the relationship between humans and labor. Previously in human history, he argued, humans extracted raw materials from the environment and performed some action (labor) on those materials to produce something that could be used. Marx believed humans fulfilled their essence through this kind of work because they used creative capacities to overcome challenges imposed by nature and worked toward their collective survival. However, Marx argued, the nature of work in modern capitalism results in **alienation**, separation of humans from their essence. He further posited that under capitalism, factory workers create products not for their own use or self-expression but to make a profit for factory owners. Because workers are separated from the land and have few other options for survival, they work in factories out of necessity rather than free will. In addition, the rise of factory work led to increased *division of labor*, in which each individual played only a small role in the production process. As a result, labor was no longer a satisfactory expression, but simply a mechanical, controlled process which alienated individuals from their essence.

Marx argued that capitalism encourages factory owners to exploit their workers. **Exploitation** refers to a situation in which a person, system, or group unfairly takes advantage of another person, system, or group for personal gain. Marx believed factory owners took advantage of workers to benefit themselves at the workers' expense. In Marx's time, factory workers worked long hours on repetitive tasks for little pay. There were few labor laws, so things like minimum wage, overtime pay, and even work-free weekends did not exist. Marx believed exploitation of workers facilitated the growth of capitalism, and as capitalism grew, workers would become more and more exploited. Since the goal of capitalism is to continually increase profits, factory owners must repeatedly find new ways to cut the costs of production. Methods of cutting costs include reducing workers' wages, forcing them to work longer hours for less pay, and replacing workers altogether with machines. Because the premise of capitalism is to continually transform money into more money, Marx believed exploitation was an intrinsic part of the growth and expansion of capitalism.

Class Conflict

A **class** is a group of people who share a common economic standing in a society such as "workers." Marx believed the increasing tensions arising from the exploitation of workers would eventually result in class conflict. He envisioned a conflict extending throughout society between owners as a group and workers as a group (and not simply owners and workers of a particular factory). He called the small class of capitalist owners the **bourgeoisie** and the large class of exploited workers the **proletariat**. Marx believed that as capitalism grew, the bourgeoisie would continue to find new ways to increase profits— through improvements in technology, increased automation, decreased wages, outsourcing, and so on— which would inevitably result in lower income and higher unemployment among the proletariat. He predicted the wealth and power of the bourgeoisie would continue to increase, while the labor and living conditions of the proletariat would continue to decline.

Marx also predicted that the exploited workers of the proletariat would eventually reach a point where they would become intolerant of increasing inequality between the classes and would revolt against the bourgeoisie to transform the capitalist system. However, he believed it would take a long time for the proletariat to reach this point of revolt, partly because proletarians were so occupied by their struggle to earn enough money to survive that they scarcely had time to consider their condition or recognize the power they could gain by organizing as a class. Workers also competed with each other for jobs, which prevented them from unifying. In addition, Marx believed that each economic system corresponds to an **ideology**, a set of beliefs and understandings about the world that systematically misrepresents, and therefore justifies, the economic system in place. In capitalism, the ideas that humans are innately selfish and greedy, competition is inevitable, and the economic system is outside human control are some components of the ideology that was keeping the system in place. Marx believed this ideology was purposely and systematically perpetuated by the bourgeoisie in multiple ways because capitalism required their control not only of the economy but also control of other social institutions, such as politics, media, religion, and family.

Despite the pervasiveness of this ideology, Marx believed that over time the proletariat would gain a sense of **class consciousness**, a recognition of their common interests. At this point, proletarians would join together and revolt against the bourgeoisie. Through class conflict, Marx believed capitalism would fall and be replaced with a new economic system. This theory of class conflict and social change is Marx's concept of *dialectical materialism*, which posits that societies progress into different stages through conflict. In this scheme, capitalism is the *thesis*, which is supported by the bourgeoisie. The proletariat supports an *antithesis*, which might be something closer to **socialism**, a system in which the government owns and operates the major institutions in society, such as education and healthcare. The two groups engage in conflict until a *synthesis* is reached, which then becomes the new economic system. The synthesis becomes the thesis, and the cycle continues until a system that provides absolute human freedom is created. Marx believed that **communism**, a classless system in which the means of production are collectively owned, was the final stage of this cycle.

There are many ideas today about what communism means and how it works, most of which are not the same as what Marx meant when he wrote about it. According to Marx, the main goal of communism is the elimination of private property. Knowing most of the population (the proletariat) already did not own any property, Marx was referring to the private ownership by the capitalists, specifically factories and other means of production. Marx believed centralizing ownership of the means of productions would result in cooperation instead of competition and fulfillment instead of alienation. Marx used the example of hunter-gatherer societies to explain his vision of a communist society. In hunter-gatherer societies, there was no private property because tribes had to move around depending on the availability of food. All labor was done with the specific goal of helping the tribe survive, so work was fulfilling and these societies were classless. Marx believed society would eventually return to a classless state after a series of struggles. At this point, humans would reach absolute political and economic freedom. In this new, classless society, each individual would contribute to society according to his or her ability and take from society according to his or her need.

EMILE DURKHEIM

Emile Durkheim (1858–1917) helped establish sociology as a distinct field of study. He sought to explain theories and concepts that distinguish sociology from its philosophical and psychological roots. Durkheim believed sociology should be modeled after the natural sciences. He developed quantitative research methods, which use the principles of science to study society.

Durkheim argued sociology should seek to understand how societies function as a whole. By stepping back from the individual to study society in its entirety, he laid the groundwork for a branch of sociological theory called *structural functionalism*. Structural functionalism views society as a structure made up of interconnected parts that work together to maintain stability. In Durkheim's view, the parts that make up society are broad *structures*, such as values, norms and belief systems, and *institutions*, such as economy, politics, education, religion, and family. These parts work together to keep the society functioning.

Durkheim used the analogy of a human body to describe how society works. Parts of society, such as norms, family, and politics, are the organs of the body, which all work together towards the proper functioning of the whole. A disruption in one part of society can cause a disruption in other parts, just like an illness that attacks one part of the body can impact the functioning of other parts of the body.

Social facts and functions

Durkheim argued that sociology should be the study of social facts and social functions. *Social facts* are things that are generalizable, or occur in the same way in all societies. Social facts exist within a society and are external to and constraining of individuals, such as norms, values, and institutions. For example, because humans are born into societies with preexisting laws, laws are external to individuals. Laws were in place in the society before those individuals were born, so the laws exist outside them. Even when new laws are created, they become part of the social structure and continue to exist after their

Emile Durkheim, 1858–1917

Emile Durkheim was born on April 15, 1858, in Epinal, France. Descending from a long line of rabbis, Durkheim initially studied to be a rabbi himself but gave up on this endeavor, and on Judaism, by his teenage years. Durkheim was frustrated with his education, believing it did not emphasize scientific methods strongly enough; as a result, he declined a career in philosophy in hopes of gaining more scientific training. In 1887 Durkheim married Louise Dreyfus, with whom he had two children, Andre and Marie. Durkheim published over 15 books, many of which were geared towards establishing sociology as a discipline. He worked at the University of Bordeaux, where he founded the first sociology department in Europe. Durkheim was also active in bringing the social sciences into the general French education system. Durkheim's son Andre was killed in December of 1915 during World War I. Durkheim never recovered from this loss; in 1917 he suffered a stroke from which he never recovered. Durkheim died on November 15, 1917.

creators die. As individuals grow up, they learn to follow the laws and other social facts of their society. Sometimes individuals would prefer not to follow the laws but follow them to avoid punishment. In this way, the laws constrain individuals' behavior by limiting their actions. Individuals who break laws are labeled deviant and punished for their actions. Thus, laws, like other social facts, are external to individuals and constrain their behaviors. Durkheim argued social facts should be considered actual things, not simply ideas. He distinguished between **material social facts**, which are tangible, observable parts of society (such as technology, art, and written laws) and **nonmaterial social facts**, which are the invisible parts of society (such as morals, values, and culture).

Durkheim also analyzed social facts to determine their **social function**, their contribution to the operations and stability of the society. For example, some social functions of laws are maintaining order and establishing justice. Regardless of their content, all laws are intended to serve the same function. Once the social function is established, sociologists can study how well a structure works in a particular society.

Normal versus Pathological

Durkheim believed sociologists should evaluate whether or not a society or social fact was functioning properly. He called healthy, well-functioning social facts **normal** and improperly functioning social facts **pathological**. He developed three rules to determine whether a social fact was normal or pathological.

The first rule is that a social fact is normal when it is the average occurrence for a given society of a given species, taking phase of development into consideration. For example, an average 35-year-old man in U.S. society could be expected to exhibit the normal social fact of acting as a father because that is an average occurrence for many 35-year-old American men. However, an average six-year-old boy, at a lower stage of development, could not be expected to do the same. The second rule is that the first rule can be verified simply through observation. If most 35-year-old men in a given society are fathers, then the social fact of being a father is normal.

The third rule is that it is especially important to make general observations of social beings when a species is not fully evolved. This point is important because it helps establish that there are differences between species as well as between societies within the same species. Durkheim meant that social facts are not normal or pathological in and of themselves but relative to the society in question. It is therefore important to apply the three rules before evaluating a social fact. For example, male elephants do not aid in raising young elephants, so for male elephants it would be pathological to behave like fathers whereas this behavior is normal for the 35-year-old American male. In other words, sociologists cannot gauge whether a social fact is normal or pathological based on their own societies. Instead, each social fact must be analyzed according to the particular characteristics of the species, group, or society being studied.

Durkheim argued that social facts are normal when they benefit the functioning of society as a whole, even if they are not considered good by individuals. An example is crime. Durkheim argued even though criminals exhibit pathological behavior, crime itself is normal because crime is necessary for society to function. He pointed out that crime exists in every society, making it an average occurrence, and concluded that it must serve a useful function. He believed the function of crime is to help societies define which behaviors are right and wrong and to then determine how to judge and treat criminals. Though most people agree crime is bad, by virtue of its regularity, it is considered normal in Durkheim's classification.

Social Solidarity

Durkheim also analyzed **social solidarity**, the ways in which societies are held together. He wanted to understand how members of society see themselves as part of a whole. Durkheim classified two types of societies based on cohesion. The first type is **mechanical solidarity** in which society is unified by individuals' similarities. People in mechanical societies share many of the same qualities and value is placed on sameness, which promotes unity. The second type is **organic solidarity** in which society is unified by individuals' differences. People in organic societies value individuality and gain unity by making use of unique strengths. Social cohesion is created in organic societies through individuals' interdependence.

The United States, which has a population that includes an enormous variety of ethnicities and nationalities, exhibits organic solidarity. There is also a great deal of variation between social classes in the United States, and value is placed on individuality. In Japan, most people share a similar ethnic background and nationality. The Japanese place more value on status and honor than class, so there is less of a gap between classes based on income than there is in the United States. Unity in Japan is derived from shared ethnicity, nationality, and class, resulting in strong mechanical solidarity.

Durkheim analyzed mechanical and organic solidarity in *The Division of Labor in Society*. As societies transitioned from agriculture- to industrial-based economies during the Industrial Revolution, division of labor increased. Some social scientists worried this division of labor was breaking down social solidarity as people embraced individuality and focused less on their sameness. Durkheim argued that solidarity was not decreasing, merely changing. Whereas agricultural societies had strong mechanical solidarity, the division of labor spurred by increasing industrialization allowed organic solidarity to develop.

Suicide

Durkheim examined social solidarity further in his study of suicide. Durkheim's study of suicide used *quantitative research methods*, a research approach that uses numbers and statistics. He demonstrated how sociologists could use numbers and statistics to study social phenomena. He also demonstrated the unique perspective sociologists could offer to the broader scientific knowledge base. Durkheim studied suicide because suicide is often viewed as a highly personal, individualistic act that can only be understood through psychological analysis. He demonstrated that there were social patterns in suicides based on individuals' levels of connectedness with the society.

Durkheim used quantitative sociological analysis to identify four types of suicide. *Egoistic suicide* occurs when an individual has weak ties to society and experiences social isolation. For example, Durkheim found individuals who lived alone were more likely to commit suicide than those who lived with families. *Anomic suicide* also results from weak ties to society, particularly situations in which individuals feel a lack of regulation from society. Durkheim found higher rates of suicide in times of economic downturn and economic boom. He concluded that sudden change in one's economic situation can lead to confusion over the rules associated with the new status. *Altruistic suicide* occurs when individuals have such close ties to society that they give up their lives to benefit others in the social group. An example of altruistic suicide is suicide bombers who give up their lives to make a political statement they believe will benefit their society's people. *Fatalistic suicide* occurs when individuals are so strongly regulated by society they feel they have no freedom or independence. These individuals turn to suicide as the only way to escape their situation (for example, suicide among African American slaves). Through his identification of these four types of suicide, Durkheim demonstrated that suicide is not only psychological but also sociological.

SUMMARY

Auguste Comte, Harriett Martineau, Karl Marx, and Emile Durkheim are some of the founders of sociology. These theorists, who were mainly writing at a time when sociology did not yet exist, worked to develop sociology as a discipline. They worked to define the subject matter of the discipline, create its theoretical and methodological approaches, and envision the place of sociology in the broader spectrum of academic knowledge.

Further Reading

Cuff, E.C., W.W. Sharrock, and D.W. Francis. *Perspectives in Sociology,* 5th ed. London: Routledge, 2006.

Kimmel, Michael S. *Classical Sociological Theory,* 2nd ed. New York: Oxford University Press, 2007.

Lengermann, Patricia Madoo, and Jill Niebrugge-Brantley. *The Women Founders: Sociology and Social Theory, 1830–1930.* New York: McGraw-Hill, 1998.

Ritzer, George. *Classical Sociological Theory,* 5th ed. New York: McGraw-Hill, 2008.

Turner, Jonathan H., Leonard Beeghley, and Charles H. Powers. *The Emergence of Sociological Theory,* 6th ed. Belmont, Calif.: Thomson Wadsworth, 2007.

CHAPTER 4

LATER CLASSICAL SOCIAL THEORISTS

This chapter continues the previous chapter's discussion about the classical theorists. Whereas the previous chapter summarized the work of early classical theorists, this chapter summarizes the work of later classical social theorists and covers the work of Anna Julia Cooper, Charlotte Perkins Gilman, Max Weber, and W.E.B. Du Bois.

ANNA JULIA COOPER

Anna Julia Cooper's (1858–1964) sociological work focused on the central theme of **domination**—the systematic control of one group in society by another. In situations of domination, the group that holds power is the **dominant group** and the group that lacks power is the **subordinate group**. Cooper analyzed racial domination in particular, but she argued that any fight for equality should advocate equality for all. Her sociology was intended as a form of social activism rather than a neutral observation as advocated by some of the other early theorists.

Race and the Women's Movement

In her essay "Woman versus the Indian," Cooper responded to a speech given by Anna Howard Shaw, a women's rights activist, at the National Woman's Council in 1891. Shaw argued that women should be granted **suffrage** (the right to vote) because men of color were already allowed to vote. She observed that if white men allowed black and Native American men to vote, they should allow

Anna Julia Cooper, 1858–1964

Anna Julia Haywood Cooper was born in 1858 in Raleigh, North Carolina, to Hannah Stanley Haywood, a slave, and her white master, George Washington Haywood. Cooper attended St. Augustine's Normal School and Collegiate Institute for newly freed slaves from the age of nine, eventually becoming a teacher. She taught for several years until she married George Cooper in 1877 and was forced to leave her job because married women were forbidden to work. She became a widow in 1879 and never married again. Cooper enrolled at Oberlin College where she earned bachelor's and master's degrees. She taught at the Washington Colored High School (known as the M Street School) in Washington, D.C., where she became principal. Cooper advocated advanced education for black students, an unpopular position among white elitists who, at that time, preferred vocational training for black students. Cooper was dismissed from her position at M Street in 1902 only to be called back in 1910. In 1914 she began

working toward a doctoral degree at Columbia University but had to withdraw when she adopted her half-brother's five orphaned children. Cooper later enrolled at the University of Paris-Sorbonne where she earned a Ph.D., becoming the fourth African American woman to earn that degree. Cooper was a teacher, scholar, and political activist. She wrote several books, including *A Voice from the South: By a Woman from the South*, which is credited as the first black feminist publication. She helped found the Colored Women's League of Washington, D.C., the Colored Women's YWCA, and the Camp Fire Girls. Cooper was invited to speak at the World Congress of Representative Women at the Chicago World's Fair in 1893 and the first Pan-African Conference in London in 1900. In 1964, at the age of 105, Cooper died in her sleep in Washington, D.C.

Anna Julia Cooper (AP/USPS)

white women to vote as well. Cooper responded that women should not try to gain rights at the expense of others (e.g., racial minorities). Instead, Cooper argued, the fight for women's rights should be a fight for *all* women's rights.

When equality is reached for all people, she noted, the struggle for women's rights would be victorious.

Although she did not use these terms, Cooper distinguished between **institutional racism** (systematic unequal treatment built into the fabric of society, such as segregation laws, separate restrooms, and so on) and **everyday racism** (uncivil treatment of one individual by another in face-to-face interactions). Cooper equated everyday racism with *bad manners*. She suggested that the mistreatment of one individual by another results from poorly trained citizens. She called on women to teach *good manners* and thereby work toward eradicating racism.

Cooper advocated good manners because she believed perceptions of one group as superior to another were reinforced through everyday social interactions. She argued that perceptions of whites being superior to African Americans were perpetuated through everyday acts of racism. She used an example of a white citizen reprimanding an African American for sitting in the designated "white" part of a bus. In a typical scenario, the white citizen was not likely to address the African American with respect or kindness, but instead pose a threat and demand that the African American move to another seat. Cooper argued that such a scenario, in which one ordinary citizen shows a lack of respect for another, reinforces for both individuals the broader hierarchy in society. That is, the actions remind both individuals and any witnesses that the two belong to different social groups and that one social group is dominant over the other. Cooper suggested that if everyday events of this kind were eliminated, whites might begin to see African Americans as ordinary human beings. Once this kind of ideology was in place, she contended, it would follow that laws and social policies that deny African Americans full participation in society would also change.

Cooper called on women to help eradicate racism because women in the United States were just beginning to gain a political voice through participation in the women's movement. Cooper used the analogy of a man with one eye to describe social knowledge in the United States at the time. Because U.S. society was controlled by white men, there was only one perspective or view of the world. Because only one view was available (the view from the white male perspective), this viewpoint became institutionalized. In Cooper's analogy, this single viewpoint was comparable to the one-eyed man who sees only part of the world. Extending the analogy, Cooper suggested women's inclusion in public discourse and elsewhere was comparable to a bandage being lifted from the other eye and thus allow for a clearer, more complete perspective. Because women had the opportunity to determine how their perspective would shape political discourse, Cooper requested that women take this new opportunity seriously and carefully select the message they wanted to promote.

Cooper argued that women's cause was freedom. In seeking freedom for themselves, Cooper suggested women should fight for freedom for all and advocate for other marginalized groups. In particular, women should not turn against other groups deemed subordinate in society and attempt to gain rights at their expense. She denounced feminist activists who suggested women should have the right to vote only because black and Native American men (who were presumed to be subordinate to white women in the social hierarchy) already had the right to vote. Such a stance would reinforce race subordination, and mask the true message of the women's movement which was a fight for freedom. Above all Cooper argued that the fight for women's rights should be a fight for *all* women's rights, not just white women's rights. She called on women who were active in the women's movement to fight for true justice and freedom for all.

Race and Social Change

Cooper asserted that there were two ways to ensure peace in society, the first of these being *suppression*, with the dominant group maintaining full power and the subordinate group(s) quietly and passively accepting subordination. Cooper viewed this as a negative peace, one not found in other elements of the universe. A second type of peace could be created through *conflict* between opposing groups, which Cooper considered natural and progressive because it could be found throughout the universe as opposing forces worked to find balance between them. This type of peace, she argued, is normal, healthy and necessary for the progression of society.

Cooper stated that the purpose of distinguishing between racial groups in society was to generate social conflict to produce social change. She posited that each race had a message for society. If different races never came into contact with each other, the messages would not come into conflict, and therefore would not be heard properly. Instead, there would be a simple consensus, or agreement, that would not bring about social progress. Similarly, Cooper believed that the simple domination of one group by another also hindered social progress. In the case of simple domination, only the ideas of one group could be heard. In such a scenario, a society would stagnate because there would be no opposition to the prevailing social arrangements.

It was Cooper's belief that in clashes between groups, a mutual compromise must be reached. In her view, it was compromises born of conflict that would bring society to a more advanced state. In seeking equilibrium between opposing groups, society would advance to its next phase. It was through this progression, Cooper suggested, that human freedom would eventually be reached.

CHARLOTTE PERKINS GILMAN

Charlotte Perkins Gilman's (1860–1935) sociological theory focused primarily on gender, culture, and economics. The purpose of theory for Gilman was social change. She believed sociological theory could facilitate a better understanding of human pain and that this understanding could help bring about positive social change. Although Gilman's analysis focused on women's unequal status in U.S. society, the purpose of social change for Gilman was to improve society as a whole, not just the status of women. Gilman resisted being labeled a "feminist," preferring instead the label "humanist."

Gender and Economics

In *Women and Economics* Gilman analyzed gender relations in the United States as an economic condition. She suggested that throughout the animal kingdom, all animals—including humans—are modified mostly by the activities they engage in to acquire food. Since food is the most basic need of all animals, it is through the acquisition of food that animals secure their livelihood. Applying this idea to humans, she argued that those attributes humans use to secure their economic livelihood become the most developed. For example, a person who builds houses for a living and spends time lifting heavy building materials would develop stronger arm muscles over time. On the other hand, for someone writing creative stories for a living, it would be natural to see an increased creative capacity over time. Gilman viewed these characteristic developments as both individual and collective, meaning that if a large group (or class) of people gained its livelihood through house building and another through creative writing, the house builders as a group should have greater arm strength and the writers as a group should be more creative. Moreover, the longer these two distinct groups existed, the more differentiated they would become.

Gilman used an evolutionary understanding of human characteristics based on the concept of **survival of the fittest**, the idea that the individuals in a species who have the most desirable traits will be selected for reproduction, thereby continuing and even strengthening those traits in the species. Over time, desirable traits become more prominent in the species as individuals who best exhibit the traits continue to reproduce and those who do not die out. In this way, Gilman suggested, humans are modified most by what they do for a living, and this operates on both an individual and a collective level. The broader argument Gilman was making is that social action (or society) impacts humans' physical bodies (or biology).

In her analysis of gender relations in the United States during the early 1900s, Gilman argued that humans in this social setting had a distinct economic relationship that differed from economic relationships formed by any other animal species. She used the term **sexuo-economic relation** to describe the phenomenon found among humans in which the relationship between the sexes (men and women) is an economic relationship. Gilman argued that women in U.S. society were economically dependent on men. She defined

Charlotte Perkins Gilman, 1860–1935

Charlotte Perkins Gilman was born on July 3, 1860, in Hartford, Connecticut. Her mother was Mary Perkins and her father was Frederich Beecher Perkins, a writer and nephew of Harriet Beecher Stowe. In 1866, Gilman's father left her mother after she gave birth to an infant who died. Gilman and her mother lived in poverty, often staying with various family members and in temporary housing. Gilman was mostly self-educated. She studied for two years at the Rhode Island School of Design and then designed greeting cards for a living. In 1884 she married Charles Walter Stetson, an artist. After giving birth to her first child, Katherine Beecher Stetson, Gilman suffered from depression. The common prescription for depression at the time was rest and relaxation, and Gilman's doctor recommended she live a domestic life and refrain from writing and other artistic work—a recommendation her husband agreed with and tried to enforce. In 1888 Gilman left her husband; they officially divorced in 1894. In 1902, Gilman married her cousin George Gilman, a New York attorney. During the next twenty years, Gilman became famous through her lectures and monthly journal *The Forerunner.* She also authored over 200 essays and ten books. She was diagnosed with breast cancer in 1932. Two years later her husband passed away, and Gilman moved to California to be with her daughter. On August 17, 1935, she took her own life. After her death, most of Gilman's work was overlooked until it was revived by feminist movement activists in the 1960s.

Charlotte Perkins Gilman *(Library of Congress)*

economic independence as a condition in which the economic compensation one receives is equivalent to the work done. She defined **economic dependence** as a condition in which the economic compensation one receives is based not on the work one does but on the will and ability of another. To illustrate the difference, Gilman used horses as an example. A wild horse, she explained, eats as much food as it hunts and gathers; what it gets is equivalent to the work it does. Therefore, the wild horse is economically independent. A horse owned by a human, however, is given whatever amount of food its master chooses and is able to give. This horse's economic livelihood depends not on how much work it does but on the will and ability of another. In captivity, one horse may do a lot of work and be fed little whereas another horse may do no work and be fed well. Under such conditions, the horses are economically dependent.

Gilman argued that women in U.S. society during the time she was writing were in a condition of economic dependence on men. Their roles as housewives and mothers created a situation in which the compensation they received for the work they did was not determined by the amount or quality of their work but was determined by the men they had married. In other words, a woman was economically dependent on how much her husband had and how much he chose to share with her. Thus, the compensation women received for their work was determined solely by the will and ability of another. Gilman also pointed out that women who did the most work—that is, poor women—got compensated the least for their work whereas women who did the least work—that is those who had the economic means to hire others to do housework, cook, and care for their children—got compensated the most.

Gilman argued that since women's economic dependence on men meant that they acquired their economic livelihood not through work but through marriage, the work women did to obtain economic security was securing a husband. In this way, a woman's economic function (what she did to ensure her livelihood) was a sexual function (what she did to reproduce). In other words, a woman had to find a man with whom to reproduce in order to obtain economic security, and her economic standing depended on the man she married. Sexual functions for men also became economic functions. That is, a man's ability to find a woman with whom to reproduce depended on the economic livelihood he was able to provide.

According to Gilman, the consequence of this uniquely human sexuo-economic relationship resulted in **excessive sex distinction** or exaggerated gender differences between men and women. Expanding on her argument that the activities individuals engage in to secure their livelihood modify them the most, Gilman suggested that if men and women engaged in the same activity to secure their livelihood (such as hunting or house building or creative writing), they would develop similar characteristics. But she noted that if men and women continued to engage in gender-dictated activities to secure their economic livelihood, they would continue to develop different traits and would become more and more different from each other over time.

Gilman argued that this sexuo-economic relation encouraged excessive femininity in women. She noted that girls are taught from a young age to focus on qualities that will attract a husband, such as physical beauty, slenderness, and passivity. In essence, women learned to become "the weaker sex," both physically and psychically. For men, Gilman noted, this sexuo-economic relation encouraged an emphasis on sexuality and capitalist accumulation (earning money). Because men's economic functions were sexual functions (they must earn economic security in order to obtain a sexual mate) they had become overly consumed with sexuality. Men had also, in Gilman's view, become excessively focused on capitalist accumulation, or acquiring money and wealth because a man's economic success was intertwined with his ability to secure a wife. On a societal level, Gilman suggested this resulted in an overemphasis on individual success at the expense of the social good. In other words, this sexuo-economic relationship facilitated a cultural ideology that placed value on the well-being of one's self and immediate family over the well-being of the whole society.

Gender and Culture

In *The Man-Made World, or Our Androcentric Culture*, Gilman suggested that U.S. society during her time overemphasized masculinity and femininity and ignored characteristics that are more commonly human. She argued that male dominance in U.S. society had allotted men the power to develop society and its institutions solely on "masculine" ways of being and thinking. This pattern, according to Gilman, had resulted in an **androcentric culture**, or a collective consciousness that reflected masculine ways of understanding the world. Over time, these ways of thinking and acting had come to be accepted as the norm, thereby facilitating and maintaining an ideology that defined "maleness" as "humanness." In the process, that which was "feminine" had come to be considered different, deviant, and other. Gilman argued that U.S. culture was not a reflection of human ways of thinking and interacting but of male ways of thinking and interacting. Hence, the culture itself had become androcentric, or male-dominated, and this dominance was evident in every facet of social life, including family, religion, art, literature, games and sport, government, and politics.

Gilman was critical of androcentric culture because it was built on male domination over women and reflected masculine characteristics (such as competition and domination) while minimizing feminine and human characteristics. In addition, such a culture promoted the belief that women lacked the characteristics necessary to operate in the man-made culture and institutions. Women were thus relegated to the home, where feminine characteristics were considered appropriate and useful, further ensuring the perpetuation of androcentrism. Gilman suggested that the family in an androcentric culture was a *proprietary family*, a social arrangement designed to serve men rather than children. She believed that masculine characteristics could also be identified in the prevailing political system, government, and military, all of which were based on conflict and competition rather than cooperation and compromise. Gilman argued that this style of government had created an *andocracy*, or male-run government, rather than a *democracy*, or human-run government.

To create positive social change, Gilman argued, it was necessary to create culture and institutions that reflect human rather than masculine or feminine characteristics. In such a society, laws would be viewed not as weapons of combat but as guiding principles for action. Emphasis would be placed on the common good rather than on the individual. This emphasis would call for collective solutions to problems. Such a culture would benefit not just women but society and humanity as a whole.

MAX WEBER

Max Weber (1864–1920) examined changes occurring in Western societies during the Industrial Revolution. Weber believed Western societies were undergoing **rationalization**, a process by which people's activities become more calculated, methodical, and efficient. An example of rationalization was the transition from producing goods individually to large-scale factory production. In factories, individuals worked with machines to produce far more goods than each could produce alone. This was an efficient, calculated method of producing goods, whereby the greatest number of goods could be produced with the least amount of money and human power. However, as Weber posited, maximizing production comes at a cost, as each individual's job on an assembly line is monotonous and workers may lack a sense of accomplishment and pride in the goods they produce due to their separation from the final product. Weber saw evidence of rationalization in several facets of society, including production, economics, politics, bureaucracies, science, and increasingly, everyday life. He believed social phenomena had historical causes, and he sought to create a sociology that would increase understanding of the historical causes of modern characteristics of society.

Weber's Vision of Sociology

Weber believed scientific methods were of limited use in sociology. Science, he argued, seeks to *generalize*, which requires finding phenomena that occur the same in all cases. Weber recommended that sociologists focus on the *individual case* that differs from the generality to understand how societies differ from each other, thereby illuminating the detailed workings of the society under investigation.

A methodological tool Weber created to facilitate sociological investigation was ideal types. An **ideal type** is a prototype of some phenomenon, or a list of characteristics that represent the phenomenon in its purest form. The ideal type can then be examined to uncover the historical causes of the phenomenon it represents, or it can be used as a comparison for its observable real-world counterpart. For example, a sociologist might create a list of characteristics that would make up a pure democracy—this would be the ideal type. The sociologists could then compare real-world democracies to the ideal type to study their similarities and differences. Ideal types are essentially yardsticks for sociologists to use as a comparison tool. Weber argued that ideal types should not be confused with reality. Ideal types would not be found in the real world but were merely an exaggeration that might help social scientists make sense of society. Weber also noted that ideal types do not have to be positive; a list of the worst possible characteristics could be compared to real-world situations, or a particular ideal type could be created for something negative, such as war.

Although Weber did not advocate the use of scientific methods in sociology, he did advocate *value-free sociology*—an approach in which sociologists set aside their own values and ideas about how societies *should be* and simply seek to understand *what is*. Weber used the German word *verstehen*, which means to understand, to emphasize this as the goal of sociology. He believed politicians

Max Weber, 1864–1920

Max Weber was born on April 21, 1864, in Erfurt, Germany. His parents were comfortably middle class, but Weber's home life was plagued with tension. Weber's father was a materialistic man who valued earthly pleasures. His mother was a strict Calvinist who avoided material goods in an attempt to live an ascetic life. This contrast led to marital tensions that profoundly affected Max Weber. When he was eighteen, he escaped the tension briefly to attend the University of Heidelberg. Though shy, Weber shone through hard work and intellect. While at school, he adopted a lifestyle similar to his father's. However, after a brief military service, Weber completed eight more years of study at the University of Berlin where he began to shift more towards his mother's views on life. Weber married his distant cousin Marianne Schnitger in 1893. In 1896, he began teaching at the University of Heidelberg. Just as his career was taking root, Weber had a serious argument with his father, which was followed shortly by his father's death in 1897. Weber suffered a nervous breakdown that incapacitated him for nearly seven years. In 1904 Weber returned to his academic career. Soon after, he published *The Protestant Ethic and the Spirit of Capitalism*, which is perhaps his most well known work. In 1919 Weber accepted a position at the University of Vienna. Only a year later he contracted a severe case of pneumonia; he died at the age of 56 on June 14, 1920.

and the general public could use the understanding of society created by sociologists to determine the course of social change.

The Protestant Ethic and the Spirit of Capitalism

Weber used his sociological method to analyze the relationship between religion and economics. In *The Protestant Ethic and the Spirit of Capitalism* Weber investigated why modern capitalism had arisen in some Western societies but not in others with similar levels of technological and economic development. In seeking to understand the causes of modern capitalism, he created an *ideal type* of the thought processes that underlie the capitalist system. Weber noted that people in modern capitalism value work and profit seeking for their own sake rather than as a means to a different end, such as survival, comfort, or relaxation. Capitalists worked hard and acquired money, not to spend on luxury items but to reinvest to make more money. This process of accumulating wealth for the sole purpose of accumulation was viewed not as greedy or selfish but as morally righteous. Weber called this moralized view of profit seeking the *spirit of capitalism.*

Weber looked to religion as an explanation for these views and values because modern capitalism had risen particularly in nations where the majority of the population was Protestant. In societies with mixed religious groups, a majority of successful capitalists were Protestant. To understand the relationship between the two, Weber examined the ideas embedded in different religions and compared them to the ideas embedded in capitalism. A popular form of Protestantism in Weber's time was Calvinism, based on the teachings of John Calvin. Calvinists believed in *predestination*, that salvation or damnation is decided by God before individuals are born and therefore cannot be altered by a person's actions. Although Calvinists had no control over whether or not they were chosen for salvation, they believed God provided signs to let them know their fate. The sign that one was chosen was living a virtuous life, which meant rejecting excessive spending and self-indulgence. Calvinists also believed opportunities were gifts from God and signs of salvation. Not accepting an opportunity was the same as rejecting a gift from God, a sign of damnation. Therefore, if a Calvinist were presented with an opportunity—a gift from God—acceptance of that opportunity was a sign of salvation. Those who earned a significant amount of money through these opportunities were forbidden to spend the money on frivolous or luxury items. Instead, the money earned presented a new opportunity—another gift from God—that could be invested to make more money. The result of this set of ideas was a group of people who worked hard and continually reinvested their money to make more money. This behavior and the choices that guided it was referred to as the *Protestant ethic.*

Weber concluded that the ideas in Protestantism, or the Protestant ethic, complimented the ideas of modern capitalism, or the spirit of capitalism.

Therefore, the Protestant ethic facilitated the growth of modern capitalism. Weber's understanding of the ethic of amassing money, choosing not to spend the money on frivolous things, and investing in further capital, which generated even more money to be re-invested, can be likened to Karl Marx's money-commodity-money (M-C-M) exchange, one of the legs capitalism stands on. However, the M-C-M exchange, or production, cannot exist without its counterpart, consumption. Without consumption of material goods, there would be no demand for their production. Though Protestantism promoted an ascetic lifestyle, this actually led to an increase in material goods as those who lived by the Protestant ethic continually invested in more production. Weber described the result as an **iron cage**, the trap of materialism humans find themselves in under a capitalistic system. Although the desire for material goods is supposed to be easily cast aside, the nature of the capitalist system affords material goods a powerful hold over humans, thus trapping them in an iron cage of consumption and materialism.

Although Weber believed Protestantism facilitated the growth of modern capitalism, he did not believe it was necessary to keep capitalism going. Weber suggested that over time the spirit of capitalism would take on a life of its own and exist independent of religious ideas.

Social Stratification and Authority

Weber also analyzed **social stratification**—the ranking of society's members in a hierarchy—and authority. He argued that stratification is based on a combination of class, status, and party. *Class* is a social ranking based on economic power, or money and is determined by income and other assets such as businesses, houses, and investments. **Status** is prestige or honor recognized by others. Whereas class may be measured by income, status refers to subjective characteristics such as community standing or family history. People in a certain status group often engage in similar activities, socialize with others in that group, and develop group attitudes and behaviors. Consequently, some individuals may enjoy high status even if they lack material wealth. However, the two are often related, as individuals' class often determines whether or not they can participate in high-status activities. A **party** is a group that organizes in pursuit of power. The goal of parties is to attain power and control over other members of society, particularly through politics. An example of a party is a political party, such as the Democratic Party, but party can be used more broadly to include special-interest groups such as the National Organization for Women (NOW) or the National Association for the Advancement of Colored People (NAACP). According to Weber, class, status, and party combined in different ways to determine social stratification.

Weber defined **authority** as power over others, or the likelihood that a group of people will obey a command from a particular figure (such as an individual) or entity (such as a state). For example, a government whose laws are consistently ignored by its citizens would have a low amount of authority whereas a government whose laws are consistently followed would have a high amount of authority. Weber observed that in order for a person or government to have authority, the power would have to be viewed as *legitimate*, or worthy, by the people governed by the authority. In studying authority, Weber observed three mechanisms that provided the needed legitimacy and corresponded with three types of authority: charismatic, traditional, and rational legal.

Charismatic authority is derived from an individual's personality. People with charismatic authority are easy to identify with, inspirational, and effective leaders. Charismatic leaders typically proclaim themselves leaders and independently generate a group of followers. Charismatic authority often emerges during times of crisis when people are looking for a strong leader to guide them through a difficult time. Examples of charismatic leaders are Adolf Hitler, Martin Luther King, Jr., and Mahatma Gandhi. These leaders were not born or elected into positions of power but attracted followers because of their charismatic personalities and inspirational speaking skills. **Traditional authority** is based on customs or habits. Traditional authority is accorded to a person or body because it has been allocated that way in the past. Traditional authority is often based on family lineage. Examples of traditional authority are kings and emperors who acquire power because they are born into positions of power or men in male-dominated households who gain power because of their gender. **Rational-legal authority** is derived from standard procedure. An example of rational-legal authority is a political figure, such as a president, senator, or governor, who is elected according to preestablished rules. Weber believed that rationalization of societies led to the dominance of rational-legal authority.

W.E.B. DU BOIS

W.E.B. Du Bois (1868–1963) studied the plight of black people in America during the late 19th and early 20th centuries. Du Bois used a multimethod approach that combined in-depth interviews, participant observation, and official statistics to create a comprehensive examination of racial inequality. He demonstrated that systematic racism against black Americans resulted in fewer job opportunities, which in turn resulted in higher unemployment and crime rates in black communities. He also illustrated the highly organized structure of social life within an urban black community.

Double Consciousness

Du Bois argued that blacks in the United States had to struggle to maintain pride in their African heritage and fit in with mainstream America. He contented that it was difficult for blacks to merge their African and American identities because fitting in with mainstream Americanism entailed identifying with white European culture, which often viewed African cultures negatively. Du Bois asserted that the result of this was **double consciousness**, a state of internal conflict stemming from being black and American characterized by a sense of having to view the world in two ways and being viewed by the world in two ways.

Double consciousness, according to Du Bois, shaped African Americans' sense of self. Whites viewed blacks as a social problem, and blacks were aware of this perception. Because they had to operate within a predominantly white

W.E.B. Du Bois, 1868–1963

William Edward Bughardt Du Bois was born in 1868 in Great Barrington, Massachusetts. Growing up in New England afforded Du Bois more opportunities than many African Americans of his time had, however, he still experienced racial discrimination. Despite this obstacle, Du Bois attended college at Fisk University and was the first African American to earn a Ph.D. from Harvard University. Du Bois completed a postdoctoral research fellowship at the University of Pennsylvania and spent most of his career working at Atlanta University. He published numerous articles, essays, and books, and was a civil rights activist. He was a founder of the National Association for the Advancement of Colored People (NAACP) and director of NAACP publications and research. Du Bois believed African Americans needed to obtain higher education to conduct social research that could support programs and policies to resolve racial inequality. By the end of his career, Du Bois was increasingly critical of American capitalism and pessimistic about America's ability to end social injustice. He moved to Ghana where he became a citizen and passed away in 1963.

W. E. B. Du Bois *(Wikipedia)*

society where exposure to white ways of thinking were inherent in everyday interactions and embedded in social institutions, they learned how to see the world through the perspective of whites. But in this ability to see the world from a white perspective, African Americans also began to view themselves as a social problem. In contrast, Du Bois noted, whites were unable to see African Americans from a black perspective and saw only their blackness. The blackness they saw functioned as a **veil** that prevented whites from seeing blacks for who they were as people.

Du Bois explained that African Americans gained a different sense of self through interactions within black families and communities, social settings in which individuals are identified by their relationships with others, by the work they do, and by their roles in the local community. Here blacks were not viewed through a veil; what was seen was social roles and personal characteristics. According to Du Bois, such interactions led to another, separate sense of self.

Du Bois argued that the result of living in a state of double consciousness resulted in inner conflict and turmoil, particularly because of the negative views of blacks held by whites. He proposed that the solution to this inner conflict was for blacks to embrace their African heritage with pride and still be American, without making either identity subordinate to the other.

Race and Capitalism
Du Bois extended Karl Marx's theory of capitalism in *Black Reconstruction in America*, a work that supported the idea that racial oppression was fundamental to capitalism. Du Bois believed that competition for jobs in the South after emancipation was a root cause of white animosity toward blacks during Reconstruction. Most Southern whites were poor; only a small group had been wealthy enough to own slaves and plantations, but Du Bois argued that the white bourgeoisie purposely encouraged animosity between poor whites and blacks during the days of slavery and even after emancipation. Poor whites, for example, were hired as overseers or slave drivers. This slight power differential between poor whites and blacks pitted the two groups against each other, which gave poor whites a false sense of superiority and discouraged the two groups from uniting against the bourgeoisie. Du Bois posited that this resistance to unite with blacks kept poor whites at the mercy of rich whites and facilitated the continuation of capitalism. In this way, Du Bois argued racism played a significant role in the development and continuation of capitalism.

Religion in the Black Community
Du Bois also analyzed the role of religion in the black community. In *The Negro Church,* he described how the church played a pivotal role in the black

community by fulfilling not only people's spiritual needs but also communal and social needs. He examined the church as a social center that served as a social, political, and educational institution. As a social institution, the church facilitated social solidarity and support networks and provided space for individuals to build families, communities, and business relationships. As a political institution, the church operated as a site for political awakening and racial consciousness. As an educational institution, the church taught group values and morals and served as a site where blacks could learn trades and business skills and engage in business networking activities.

In his writings, Du Bois also acknowledged black women who played a central role in the black churches. Although churches were typically run by black men, black women were involved in leadership positions and maintained a strong voice in the way churches functioned. Through their work in the church, Du Bois explained, black women were integral in empowering the black community.

While lauding the positive aspects of black religious life and black churches, Du Bois was aware that some aspects of religion could be detrimental for blacks in the United States. He was particularly critical of "white Christianity," which he argued was filled with hypocrisy, particularly with respect to black Americans. Christianity, he observed, preaches love for all people, and yet whites had used Christianity to justify slavery and racial oppression.

Nondenominational churches, which make up about 12 percent of U.S. churches, often center around a charismatic preacher.

SUMMARY

Anna Julia Cooper, Charlotte Perkins Gilman, Max Weber, and W.E.B. Du Bois continued the efforts of earlier theorists to define the content and methods of sociology. These theorists also worked to develop sociological understandings of society, capitalism, and social inequality. The classical theorists who wrote in the 1800s and early 1900s shaped the discipline of sociology. Their ideas remain important in understanding how societies work today.

Further Reading

Cuff, E.C., W.W. Sharrock, and D.W. Francis. *Perspectives in Sociology,* 5th ed. London: Routledge, 2006.

Kimmel, Michael S. *Classical Sociological Theory,* 2nd ed. New York: Oxford University Press, 2007.

Lengermann, Patricia Madoo, and Jill Niebrugge-Brantley. *The Women Founders: Sociology and Social Theory, 1830–1930.* New York: McGraw-Hill, 1998.

Ritzer, George. *Classical Sociological Theory,* 5th ed. New York: McGraw-Hill, 2008.

Turner, Jonathan H., Leonard Beeghley, and Charles H. Powers. *The Emergence of Sociological Theory,* 6th ed. Belmont, Calif.: Thomson Wadsworth, 2007.

CHAPTER 5

THREE MAJOR PARADIGMS

Sociological theories written after the 1930s are generally considered contemporary theories. Much contemporary sociological theory can be classified into three major paradigms. A **paradigm** is a broad set of ideas, or a general conception about how things work. The three major paradigms in sociology are structural functionalism, conflict thery, and symbolic interactionism. Structural functionalism has roots in the classical works of Emile Durkheim and Herbert Spencer. Conflict theory is rooted in the classical works of Karl Marx and Max Weber. Symbolic interactionism emerged in the 1960s, and is based on the works of philosophers and psychologists from the University of Chicago.

STRUCTURAL FUNCTIONALISM

Structural functionalism primarily focuses on social consensus and equilibrium. *Consensus theories* view society as an entity characterized by collective agreement and harmony. A component of consensus in structural functionalism is the view that there are agreed upon norms, values, and goals that the collective strives to maintain. Structural functionalism also emphasizes societal **equilibrium**, a state in which opposing forces balance each other to attain stability. Structural functionalists view society as a stable, organized system of interrelated parts. All parts work together in cooperation to make society run smoothly.

Talcott Parsons

Talcott Parsons (1902–1979) was an American sociologist known for developing structural functionalism. Parsons synthesized and expanded upon the works of classical theorists Emile Durkheim and Max Weber to form a comprehensive structural functionalist theory. His analysis began with an examination of human action on the *micro level*, the level of everyday life. Parsons argued that people interact to achieve *unit acts*, or goals. He believed for social order to exist, human interaction must include *status roles*, expectations for individuals' behavior depending on the social role they are fulfilling. Parsons viewed status roles as aspects of a **system**—a complex whole formed by related parts—that are external to individuals. For example, the status of doctor in U.S. society is viewed as prestigious and carries an expectation of professionalism. According to Parsons, this status role originates in the social structure rather than the imagination of individuals. Further, Parsons argued status roles vary across societies and are based on cultural values and norms. For example, police officers are viewed as respectable in some countries and corrupt in others. Parsons viewed status roles as part of a behavior system, which he argued works together with culture, structure, and personality to maintain social order.

Parsons explained the integration of culture, structure, personality, and behavior through his theory of the *action system*. He argued four specific functions—adaptation, goal attainment, integration, and latency (AGIL)—must be achieved for the system to run smoothly. **Adaptation** means a system must be able to extract from its existing environment to meet its needs. **Goal attainment** occurs when a system is based on specific goals and provides universal definitions. **Integration** is the function that overseas and directs the achievements and relationships between the other three functions (A, G, & L). Integration maintains relationships and repairs broken ones. **Latency** is the function that allows the system to continue existing even when people are not actively maintaining it. For latency to occur, people must have motivation and cultural norms to maintain the existing system. For example, although people do not go to school all day or every day, the value of education and the school system in general continues to exist when people are at home, visiting with family, or at work.

Parsons applied AGIL to the systems he originally declared as essential for social order: behavioral, personality, social, and cultural. He argued that each system fulfills one function of AGIL. Adaptation occurs in the behavioral system. Goal attainment takes place in the personality system, which is controlled by the social and cultural systems. Integration occurs in the social system, which regulates social order through mechanisms such as teaching social norms and values. As in the personality system, individuals have little ability to change the values and norms of the society in the social system. Latency occurs

The Sick Role

Consistent with Parsons's view that status roles originate in the structure of society, he argued that when individuals become ill they are expected to behave in accordance with the socially proscribed "sick role." According to Parsons, the sick role in the U.S. originates in our cultural view of the body as an instrument. For example, individuals are expected to engage in work, which requires certain demands on the body. A sick body interferes with an individual's ability to fulfill expected roles. In such cases, the body does not fulfill its instrumental purpose. Because illness is a regular occurrence among humans that interferes with individuals' abilities to perform their expected tasks, a socially proscribed set of expectations for illness emerge. The sick role in the United States entails the privileges of being exempt from performing regular tasks, such as work, school, or childrearing. The sick role also prescribes that individuals are not personally responsible for their illness. However, Parsons argued the sick role also entails certain obligations. The individual who is ill is expected to want to recover, to seek medical attention, and to follow the recommendations of medical personnel in order to achieve recovery. In addition, sick individuals are expected to refrain from regular activities until they become well. Parsons argued the sick role is not universal but reflects the value systems and views of the body embedded in each culture.

Despite obvious ailment, this individual is also performing the sick role. *(Wikipedia)*

in the cultural system, which Parsons viewed as the most powerful since it often controls the other systems. The cultural system mediates actors within society, holds all of society's symbols and subjective meanings, and institutionalizes them through school, family, and religion. Parsons saw culture as the force that caused individuals to internalize society's norms, values, and symbols in the personality system and institutionalized them in the social system. Parsons viewed individuals as passive actors within this system.

Parsons' application of AGIL is apparent in his broader theory of society. Parsons argued society is made up of multiple parts that function together to create a smoothly running system. This is a **macro level** view of society, one that focuses on broad, overarching structures such as culture and institutions. Parsons focused specifically on four **subsystems** (parts within a larger system) of society: the economy, polity (political system), fiduciary system (family and school), and societal community (laws, media, and religious systems). He argued that *economy* helps society adapt to the environment. This requires people to work to extract resources from the environment for production and distribution of goods needed for survival. In American society the primary form of the economy is a market system. Parsons argued that the *political system* organizes members of society to contribute to the system to reach defined goals of the society. After goals are defined, integration must be met through *societal community*, or legal regulation, such as laws and police activity, and agents such as media. This legitimates society's goals and helps individuals define them as valid. Parsons also posited that the latency function depends on the *fiduciary system*. In the fiduciary system, school and family socialize children to accept cultural norms and values so that societal goals are maintained. Parsons believed that if social order were to exist each function of the AGIL action system must be met and there must be balanced exchanges between each function.

Although Parsons primarily focused on social order, he also examined social change. Parsons viewed social change as evolutionary rather than revolutionary. In connection with this, Parsons believed societies change slowly over time as they adapt to new structures and environmental arrangements. However, he believed the basic core values and norms of a society remain intact. For example, in American society, the constitution has remained fairly unchanged even though there have been significant social changes throughout the history of the United States. Parsons also viewed change as functional and necessary for a society to continue to exist. In his view, as one system in a society changes, it will cause other systems to change to establish equilibrium.

Robert Merton

Robert Merton (1910–2003) extended and revised Parson's functionalist view of society. Merton argued that functions in society can be positive or negative and that there can be multiple levels of functional analysis. In contrast to Parsons' ideas, most of Merton's research examined how structures are dysfunctional rather than functional for society. For example, whereas Parsons and other conservative structural functionalists see social inequality as functional for society, Merton argued social inequality is dysfunctional for society. A classic example of this difference is their analyses of slavery in the United States. Conservative functionalists argued slavery was necessary for the development of the U.S. economy. Merton viewed slavery as dysfunctional, as it was oppressive and dehumanizing for the individuals forced into slavery.

Merton did not believe all parts of a system integrate to create equilibrium; in his view, some functions create disorganization and disrupt social unity. Merton agreed that people are socialized in society through cultural values and norms to achieve collective objectives, a concept Parsons outlined in AGIL. However, Merton argued that not everyone in society is able to gain the means to achieve these collective goals and norms. In order to reach these goals, some people resort to **deviance**, behavior that is considered unacceptable and perhaps illegal. Thus, whereas Parsons saw collective norms and goals as functional features of a society, Merton saw their potential dysfunction.

Because Merton saw dysfunctions in society, he that argued structural functionalism needs to include *middle range theories*, theories that address specific areas within society such as poverty, drug addiction, and racism. An example of middle range theory is Merton's analysis of deviance and anomie. **Anomie** occurs when there is a disjunction between societal goals and norms and the structural ability for all members in society to achieve them. Merton argued anomie occurs in the United States when members of society cannot achieve the American cultural goal of material success because of structural constraints such as poverty and limited access to quality education. Individuals may resort to acts of deviance as a result of their inability to attain cultural goals through acceptable means. In other words, the state of anomie can lead individuals to acts of deviance.

Merton also developed the concepts of manifest and latent functions. **Manifest functions** are obvious and intended outcomes. **Latent functions** are unintended outcomes. For example, the manifest function of a prison is to punish and rehabilitate people who violate laws. The latent function is that the system provides stable employment for prison workers. Millions of jobs grow as the prison system grows and requires additional correction and parole officers, counselors, guards, and so forth. Merton argued latent functions must be functional for society rather than dysfunctional. He also believed that not all functions in society need to exist for society to continue. For example, in contrast to many other structural functionalists who viewed discrimination and inequality as functional for society, Merton believed society would continue to function if discrimination were eliminated.

CONFLICT THEORY

Although conflict theory originated in the work of Karl Marx and was also present in the works of Max Weber and other classical theorists, contemporary conflict theory emerged largely in response to structural functionalism. Where structural functionalists view society as maintaining equilibrium and stability, conflict theorists view society as characterized by inequality, conflict, and change. There are many varieties of conflict theory, and they are sometimes referred to by their classical sociological roots (for example, neo-Marxian or neo-Weberian conflict theories). Here we summarize the work of Ralf Dahrendorf, whose conflict theory responded directly to structural functionalism, and Immanuel Wallerstein, who used a neo-Marxian approach to study the world economic system.

Ralf Dahrendorf

Much of Ralf Dahrendorf's (1929–2009) conflict theory was a response to structural functionalism. Dahrendorf argued that society is characterized by consensus and conflict and that sociology needs to study both. Whereas structural functionalists argued society is characterized by consensus, social integration, and stability, Dahrendorf argued it is equally characterized by conflict, disintegration, and change. Dahrendorf also believed that order is maintained not through social solidarity and consensus but by coercion of the powerless by the powerful.

In Dahrendorf's view, some people are granted *authority* (power over others) in society. Thus, he saw society as a compilation of *imperatively coordinated associations*, a set of hierarchical relationships among people. Although Dahrendorf acknowledged different levels of power within the broader society, he pointed out that any single association can be viewed in dichotomous terms, where each individual is either dominant or subordinate. According to Dahrendorf, this distribution of power is embedded not in the individuals themselves but in the social positions they occupy. Accordingly, because society is made up of multiple hierarchical associations, the same individual can be dominant in one relationship and subordinate in another.

Dahrendorf suggested that individual groups within associations hold different *interests*, or sets of goals, they deem beneficial. Typically, group interests are contradictory, meaning that whatever one group wants another group does not want. These contradictory interests can lead to social conflict. Dahrendorf argued that a dominant group is most often interested in maintaining the status quo, or keeping the power arrangements the same. In contrast, a subordinate group is most often interested in creating social change to acquire more power so that it can become at least equal to the dominant group. Dahrendorf posited that individuals within these groups do not need to be aware of the group interests to act in accordance with them. He explained this by distinguishing between **latent interests** (interests individuals are not aware of) and **manifest interests** (interests individuals are aware of and actively working for). An example is using social networking to gain employment. Many jobs are filled through word of mouth without being advertised. When a company is hiring, people who work within the company think of people they know who are qualified for the job and may contact and encourage those people to apply. Since whites are already employed at higher rates and in higher positions than blacks and other minorities, and because whites most frequently network with other whites, this form of hiring systematically gives whites an advantage over racial minorities.

A Black Panther convention at the Lincoln Memorial in 1970. *(Library of Congress)*

However, whites do not need to be aware of this systematic advantage to perpetuate it; they are simply responding to a job opportunity that has come their way. In other words, when whites take advantage of job opportunities they learn about from people in their social networks, they perpetuate racial inequality by acting within the framework of latent interests.

Dahrendorf identified three types of groups: quasi groups, interest groups, and conflict groups. A *quasi group* is a set of individuals who fill similar social positions and therefore share common role interests. A quasi group might be members of a particular social class or members of a specific race. An *interest group* is a group of individuals who recognize their common interests and join together to advocate social change. Groups such as the Black Panthers, the National Organization for Women (NOW), and the American Civil Liberties Union (ACLU) are examples of interest groups. Interest groups are made up of individuals from quasi groups, but not everyone in the quasi group will choose to join an interest group. A *conflict group* is a group of individuals who actually engage in conflict with an opposing group. A conflict group can be made up of individuals from different interest groups who are willing to join together and engage in conflict to create change. Dahrendorf believed that once conflict groups are created, they act in ways that result in changes to the social structure.

Immanuel Wallerstein

Immanuel Wallerstein (1930–) is considered a neo-Marxian theorist because he drew upon Marx's theories and concepts and employed a historical approach to further understand the nature and impact of the economic system. Wallerstein analyzed economics in terms of a *world system*, a broad social system that transcends political and national boundaries. He argued that this system is bound by a variety of competing forces, which have the potential to cause the system's eventual demise.

Wallerstein distinguished between two types of world systems: world empires and world economy. A **world empire** exists when one or a few countries take political control over others, usually through military conquest. Conquered societies are typically able to remain relatively autonomous in their operations as long as they continue to provide natural resources to the dominant empire. Wallerstein believed world empires were the primary form of relationships between societies before the capitalist revolution began in the 1400s. A **world economy** exists when a group of nations maintain economic control over others. In Wallerstein's view, the years between 1450 and 1640 were characterized by a shift from military control of power to economic control of power. He saw economic control as more efficient and more humane than military control.

In Wallerstein's analysis of the capitalist world economy, he classified nations into three categories: core, periphery, and semi-periphery. *Core* nations are dominant nations that maintain the greatest amount of wealth and power. Wallerstein suggested that core nations work in much the same way that Marx described the *bourgeoisie*, or capitalist class—by creating wealth through exploitation of subordinates. *Periphery* nations are less developed nations whose resources are exploited by core nations. Periphery nations are comparable to Marx's *proletariat*, or exploited working class. *Semi-periphery* nations are those that fall between periphery and core nations; they are the least developed core nations and the most developed periphery nations. Semi-periphery nations often mediate trade between core and periphery nations.

Wallerstein posited that the primary relationships in the capitalist world economy are between the core and periphery nations. Core nations, such as the United States and Japan, are characterized by large corporations that trade with peripheral states, high levels of technology, wealth accumulation, and a consumer demand for luxury items. Periphery nations, such as Mexico and Guatemala, are characterized by a lack of economic development, poor infrastructures (such as transportation and communication), and political instability. Ongoing relations between core and periphery nations in the world economy work to maintain each group's economic status. Core nations rely on periphery nations for labor and natural resources. Prompted by their depressed economic conditions, periphery nations provide labor and resources at low prices and rely on core nations to purchase them. Core nations exploit the instability of periphery nations and engage in trade agreements that transfer even more wealth to core nations. Periphery nations continue to lack the means to develop their infrastructure, technology, and educational systems, so they remain poor. Furthermore, individuals within periphery nations view children as workers for the family, so fertility rates are high in periphery nations, leading to overpopulation. Overpopulation further strains limited resources, perpetuating poverty and political instability.

Just as Marx predicted for capitalism in general, Wallerstein predicted the capitalist world economy would eventually come to an end. Wallerstein suggested the economic system must first permeate the entire world. Because capitalism requires ever-expanding markets, as Marx pointed out, it will eventually reach a point at which expansion is no longer possible. At this point, according to Wallerstein, the capitalist system will begin to collapse. Economic strain will create conflict, which will lead to the creation of a more equitable distribution of goods and resources. Wallerstein suggested this scenario could lead not only to a new economic system but might also lead to the creation of a *socialist world government*, with the entire world being governed by a single political entity.

SYMBOLIC INTERACTIONISM

Symbolic interactionism was primarily created at the University of Chicago, known as the Chicago School. Symbolic interactionism is based on a philosophical tradition known as *pragmatism*, which focused on *practical action*, specifically actions that take place in the concrete practice of everyday life. George Herbert Mead, a Chicago School philosopher and psychologist, developed the pragmatist view into a theory that viewed the self as a product of social interaction. The idea of the self as a social product is further explained in Charles Horton Cooley's theory of the looking-glass self. Herbert Blumer, a Chicago School sociologist and former student of Mead, later expanded Mead's theories into a comprehensive theory of society, known as symbolic interactionism. Erving Goffman, also a Chicago School sociologist, developed his own version of symbolic interactionism known as dramaturgy.

George Herbert Mead

George Herbert Mead's ideas laid the foundation for symbolic interactionism. Mead responded to psychological and philosophical theories of the self that were popular during his time. His basic premise was that the self is a social being.

Mead argued the self is made up of two parts: the I and the me. The **I** is the subjective part that acts without reflecting. It is an active subject that does things, such as eat, drink, talk, walk, and think. According to Mead, individuals are born with an I. The **me** stops to reflect on the individual, to imagine how it appears in the eyes of others. The me is considered the objective part of the self because it is the object that can be observed by oneself and others. Mead argued the me is developed through social interaction.

In order to see oneself as an object, the individual must *self reflect*, or imagine him/herself as an object that can be observed and evaluated by others. For individuals to self-reflect, Mead argued, they must be able to *take the role of the other*, or imagine how they appear to someone else. To accomplish this, an individual must be able to imagine that he or she is someone else and try to see the world as that individual other might see it. In imagining the world from someone else's perspective, the individual can imagine how that person views himself. It is through this process of imagining how one appears in the eyes of another that Mead believed individuals develop a me. Together, the I and the me make up the self.

Mead believed that individuals develop a me through two stages in childhood development, a play stage and a game stage. During the *play stage*, which begins around age two, a child pretends to be a distinct other, such as mom, dad, sister, doctor, or teacher. The child *takes the role of the other*. In doing so, the child is able to reflect on his or herself from the viewpoint of the distinct other. For example, a child playing "mother" might act out a scene in which the mother interacts with the child, perhaps using a doll or stuffed animal to represent herself. Through this type of play, the child gains the ability to view herself as an object—a being that has a concrete existence in the world—from the perspective of another individual. In this stage, the child can only play distinct others and is unable to develop a complete and organized understanding of self.

George Herbert Mead's theory would posit that these girls are developing a sense of self by playing with their Campbell Kid doll. *(Library of Congress)*

Around age six or seven, children begin to participate in more structured games. Mead argued that it is during the *game stage* that children gain a more general and complete sense of self. To participate in a baseball game a child must assume all roles required for the game at once. The child must predict what members of his own and the opposing team will do based on his moves. So in deciding whether or not to run from second to third base, the child predicts what the other players will do in each scenario and selects a move based on this prediction. Mead referred to this ability to view the world from the perspective of multiple other individuals and predict what they will do as *taking the role of the generalized other.* By *taking the role of the generalized other* in games, children develop the ability to see themselves through the eyes of the broader community. This broader community may consist of some specific others, but more importantly, it consists of a *generalized other*, which represents the community or society in general rather than a particular individual.

According to Mead, once a child has the capacity to take the role of the generalized other, that child has a me, and the development of self is complete. This is a distinctly social conceptualization of self because it requires social interaction in order to develop. In addition, the individual's ability to take the role of the generalized other encourages the individual to adhere to social expectations and **norms**, standard patterns of behavior that are considered normal in a society.

Charles Horton Cooley

Charles Horton Cooley also theorized the self as a social being in his theory of the looking-glass self. The **looking-glass self** represents the idea that individuals' self-perceptions arise through interactions with others. Cooley suggested this occurs through a three-stage process. First, the individual imagines how he or she appears in the eyes of another individual. Second, the individual imagines how that appearance is evaluated by the other individual. Third, the individual has some sort of self-feeling, such as pride or embarrassment, based on his or her perception of the other's evaluation. An important component of the looking-glass self is that the entire process takes place in the individual's imagination. Cooley suggested individuals never really know how others perceive them, but they draw conclusions about others' perceptions based on the ways people respond to them in everyday interactions. Thus, an individual's sense of self is developed through interpretations of social interactions that occur in everyday life.

Herbert Blumer

Herbert Blumer developed the ideas of Mead and others at the Chicago School into the sociological theory of symbolic interactionism. Symbolic interactionism is based on three main premises: (1) individual action is based on the meanings people have for things, (2) these meanings are derived from social interactions with others, and (3) each individual uses a process of interpretation to assign meanings to things and events. In other words, objects and events are not intrinsically meaningful; instead, meanings are created by individuals. Individuals learn through social interaction what things mean to other people. However, they do not simply take on and internalize others' interpretations of things. Instead, they engage in a process of interpretation by which they create their own meanings for things, which are impacted by, but not always exactly the same as, other people's meanings. Individuals then engage in social action, or behaviors in society, based on what things mean to them.

A central component of Blumer's theory is the idea of **agency**, individual power and free will to make something happen. The idea that individuals have agency is contrary to other sociological theories that were popular at the time. The concept of agency was particularly at odds with structural functionalism. Structural functionalism relies on the notion of **sociological determinism**, the idea that individuals' actions result from external forces and social structures rather than individual agency. The debate between the two theories is whether individuals act from free will (agency) or as a result of external forces that cause them to act in particular ways (sociological determinism). Blumer argued that individual action is based on free will, and individuals act according to how they interpret situations.

To illustrate the distinction, consider your own plans for your education. A symbolic interactionist perspective would analyze your attending a particular college as resulting from your own actions, which are based on your interpretations of various situations. From this perspective, you chose to perform well in high school and apply to a particular college because you interpreted these actions as having positive implications for your future. In this view, individuals go to college based on their own free will and personal choices, which are in part impacted by the people around them, such as parents, teachers, and friends. These individuals also choose to avoid activities that will interfere with the ability to go to college, such as crimes that could result in imprisonment.

From a sociological determinism perspective, individuals do not act based on free will but as a result of broader forces in the structure of society. Seen through the lens of this theory, you did not choose to attend college but were born into the right social position to become a college student during a historical time when most young adults go to college as opposed to doing something else, such as factory work, farm labor, or skilled craftsmanship. From this perspective, broader social forces such as the systems of education, economy, and family have acted upon you to promote the decision to go to a particular college. In this sense, your actions have been determined by the structure of society rather than personal choice.

Another distinction between sociological determinism and individual agency is that sociological determinism suggests individual action has little influence on large-scale social structures and institutions. In other words, social structures and institutions impact individuals, but individuals do not impact social structures and institutions. Conversely, Blumer's symbolic interactionism proposes that social structures and institutions are created, maintained, and changed through individual and social actions and interactions. In particular, Blumer argued that structures and institutions are created through *joint action*, scenarios in which individuals interact with one another to create action. Joint acts are not just individual isolated acts, but consist of created interactions between two or more people. Following the premises of symbolic interaction, individuals engage in joint acts as a response to their interpretations of situations. Blumer argued that it is through joint action that individuals work together to create ongoing meanings for things and patterns of action and interaction. Over time, these patterned actions and interactions develop into social structures and institutions, forming the basis of society.

According to Blumer, the result of a social action is not predetermined; it emerges through the process. That is, through the course of doing things, the way people act and the result of their actions will emerge depending on the ways a situation unfolds. This view is different from that proposed by structural

Adult Children

Symbolic interactionists argue that how people treat themselves and others is prompted by symbolic meanings they are associated with. A young boy living in a typical American family is likely to have the assigned meanings of "child," "son," and "sibling," and will behave and be treated in ways that are considered socially acceptable for children, sons, and brothers. When the boy becomes a young man and goes to college, he begins to develop an identity as an adult. A professor will expect behavior from the young man that is different from the behavior expected from a young boy because of the symbolic meaning of "college student" and "independent adult." This shift in the assigned symbolic meanings of an individual can sometimes cause tension when old meanings and new meanings overlap. When the college student visits his parents, a conflict can arise between the expectations of the parents, who still assign the meaning of "son" and "child" to the man, and the behavior of the man, who sees himself as an independent adult. Likewise, the man may struggle with the shift in the symbolic meaning of his parents. As a child, the man viewed his parents as symbols of authority and protection. As the man ages, his dependence on his parents changes, and as the man needs less actual parenting, "parent" may shift into "mentor" or "friend." This change in symbolic meaning is a common cause of friction in families as children become adults. Recognizing that people behave and treat others according to symbolic meanings can help alleviate these tensions. When a man's mother asks him a question such as "What time will you be home?" the man who is well versed in sociological theory can avoid frustration by realizing his mother is simply adjusting to the new symbolic meaning he has adopted.

functionalists who argued that social actions and their consequences are predetermined. Blumer posited that although some social acts occur every day in the same pattern, the end result may not always be the same. Therefore, an individual's course of action will vary depending on how that individual perceives a situation and how others in the interaction respond to the individual's actions. How the actions and interactions will unfold and what the consequence or benefits of the actions will be cannot be determined until the action is complete.

Erving Goffman

Erving Goffman created the symbolic interactionist theory of **dramaturgy**, which views social life as a series of performances. Goffman argued that the self is a product of social interaction and that individuals engage in a series of performances as they go about their everyday lives. The purpose of these performances is *impression management,* that is, a way of controlling the images of oneself others see. Goffman argued that individuals try to present themselves in as positive a light as possible to impact the ways others view them. Individuals, in Goffman's view, engage in impression management through their *presentation of self,* the ways they portray themselves to others.

This process, according to Goffman, requires work. Just like actors on stage, Goffman explained, individuals in everyday life rely on props and costumes to help convince their "audience" to believe their performances. For example, taxi drivers, doctors, and police officers use uniforms as symbolic markers to identify their respective positions in society and make their performances more believable. If a woman claiming to be a police officer were wearing pajamas or a bathing suit or a taxi driver's uniform, her claim might not be believed. However, if the same woman wore a police uniform, the automatic assumption would be that she is indeed what she claims to be. Her performance would be more believable based on her "costume." But as the police officer goes about her life, she does not always play the part of police officer. Consequently, she will change into different costumes depending on the role she is performing. Her different costumes are part of her presentation of self, as she may not want to be perceived as a police officer when performing other roles, such as dating partner, gym member, or parent.

Goffman also conceptualized social situations as consisting of a *front stage* and *back stage.* The *front stage* is where the performances take place whereas the *back stage* is where the preparation occurs. A restaurant is a common example, where dining and waiting areas constitute the front stage whereas kitchen and dishwashing areas make up the backstage. Hosts and servers greet and serve food to customers in the front stage, which is typically kept clean and neat. Restaurant workers engage in impression management in the front stage to portray themselves as good workers and to portray the restaurant in a positive light. This impression management might be achieved or reinforced by interactions that are polite and respectful, such as addressing customers as "sir" and "madam." Goffman pointed out the restaurant workers do not interact with each other the same way they interact with customers. Instead, they engage in a different form of impression management in the back stage, which is typically concealed from the customers' view. In the back stage, the workers perform for each other, working to portray themselves as friendly, funny, or cool.

According to Goffman's theory, individuals engage in different performances throughout their everyday lives, giving different presentations of self depending on the situations they are in. Thus, the *self* is viewed as a social being, created and shaped by social situations. Moreover, each individual has multiple selves. In Goffman's view, none of these selves is a true self or one of several fake or false selves. Instead, each self is a performance, because individuals perform multiple roles throughout their lives with each role represented by a corresponding self.

SUMMARY

Structural functionalism, conflict theory, and symbolic interactionism make up the three main paradigms in sociology. Each theory views society in a completely different way from the others and therefore asks different questions and provides different answers about any single substantive topic. For example, to study deviance, structural functionalists would examine social structure and institutions, conflict theorists would examine social inequalities and disagreements about what is considered deviant, and symbolic interactionists would examine the meanings and definitions individuals assign to actions that are considered deviant. Together, the answers provided by these three paradigms create a well-rounded view of any sociological topic.

Further Reading

Holstein, James A., and Jaber F. Gubrium. *Inner Lives and Social Worlds: Readings in Social Psychology.* New York: Oxford University Press, 2003.

Kivisto, Peter. *Social Theory: Roots and Branches*, 4th ed. New York: Oxford University Press, 2011.

Ritzer, George. *Sociological Theory*, 8th ed. New York: McGraw-Hill, 2011.

Turner, Jonathan H. *The Structure of Sociological Theory*, 7th ed. Belmont, Calif.: Wadsworth, 2003.

CHAPTER 6

SOCIAL LIFE AND
THE REALM OF IDEAS

As sociological theories continued to develop throughout the 20th century, the three main paradigms described in the previous chapter remained significant. Each theory was developed further on its own and contributed to the development of other theories. Along the lines of symbolic interactionism emerged phenomenology and ethnomethodology. Critical theory emerged as a branch of conflict theory. Phenomenology, ethnomethodology, and critical theory share an emphasis on the ideas and thought processes that impact social life.

PHENOMENOLOGY

Phenomenology was created by philosopher Edmund Husserl and developed into a sociological theory by Alfred Schutz (1899–1959). Phenomenology seeks to understand the meaning and organization of the social world through individuals' subjective experiences in everyday life. **Subjective** refers to an individual's personal interpretations, experiences, or opinions rather than an outside perspective or evidence. Because phenomenology focuses on subjectivity, it is grounded in everyday experience and attends to individuals' abilities to create the social world through interpretation. The goal of phenomenological sociology is to see the world as a society's members see it.

Life-world

Husserl argued that humans do not have direct contact with the external world. Husserl suggested individuals' personal experiences in the world are not direct experiences with a real, concrete world, but are indirect experiences mediated by consciousness. Hence, individuals experience a world that exists only through interpretations of experience.

Husserl referred to the world of human experience as the **life-world**, the world individuals sense exists. The life-world is composed of people, objects, and places that exist in each individual's perception of reality. The idea of a life-world counters the idea that there is a concrete, objective world "out there." The concept of the life-world emphasizes that the world we live in, for all *practical purposes*, is the world we perceive—a world filtered through our consciousness. Further, the life-world is taken as real by individuals. In other words, individuals assume the world they live in *is* a concrete, real world. Hence, the life-world is experienced as a real world even though it is simply an interpretation of a world—one that we can never really know is real or not.

Alfred Schutz, who expanded on the work of Husserl, argued that the life-world produces and is shaped by knowledge. That is, individuals gain knowledge through their experiences in the life-world; the knowledge individuals have subsequently shapes their life-world structures, or what they perceive to exist. Schutz suggested each social group has a **social stock of knowledge**, a set of facts and ideas available to be known. He argued that not everyone (and probably no one) has access to the entire social stock of knowledge. Instead, there is a **social distribution of knowledge** or way in which knowledge is divided among society's members. Knowledge is not divided equally because individuals have unequal access to different parts of the social stock of knowledge. In addition, most knowledge is not derived from first-hand experience but is learned from others, such as family, peers, teachers, and media.

Schutz distinguished between two types of knowledge: *knowledge about* and *knowledge of acquaintance*. These two forms of knowledge often work together but can be referred to independently. *Knowledge about* refers to the small sector of specific knowledge individuals possess. Each individual assumes some aspect of this knowledge, but the knowledge varies from person to person. This knowledge is clear, distinct, consistent, and answers the *what, how,* and *why*. This small sector of knowledge regards each individual as a "competent expert" of a personal knowledge base or specialty area. *Knowledge of acquaintance* includes the "common sense" knowledge that pretty much everyone knows. *Knowledge of acquaintance* includes only knowledge of the *what* and leaves the *how* and *why* unquestioned. For example, an individual who is familiar with using an elevator will use *knowledge of acquaintance* to operate the elevator effectively. This individual knows the elevator moves from floor to floor but does not know exactly how or why. Only an "expert" in this field of knowledge (one who has *knowledge about*) would be able to explain *how* and *why* the elevator moves from floor to floor when someone pushes a button.

A Phenomenological Study of Time and Illness

Yanqiu Rachel Zhou used phenomenological methods to capture how people in China construct the meaning of time while living with HIV/AIDS. Zhou conducted 21 in-depth interviews with people living with HIV/AIDS, following phenomenological principles throughout the study. Zhou worked to understand and describe the experiences of participants from their point of view rather than her own. She engaged in participant-led conversations during interviews that allowed participants to control the flow of information and focus on whatever issues they viewed as meaningful. Results of Zhou's study demonstrated that study participants reconceptualized the meaning of time in linear and nonlinear ways after being diagnosed with HIV/AIDS. Participants used a linear conception of time when they spoke of their future outlooks, which once were full of open-ended possibilities but were reconstructed after receiving a diagnosis with the inevitable outcome of death. A non-linear time construction was used when participants discussed family. In this context, the linear timeline of illness to death changed to a non-linear perception of the present and future. Many participants linked their lives and futures with those of other family members, which allowed for alternative frameworks of future outlooks. The present time for participants became "lived time" that focused away from illness and death and more on how to live a fulfilling life in the current moment. Zhou suggested this reconceptualization of time was therapeutic, as it allowed participants a sense of control over their present lives, which positively impacted their well-being.

Schutz argued that *knowledge of acquaintance* is mostly taken for granted in the social world. It is commonly understood by everyone and treated as "common sense." He proposed that all social groups have *knowledge of acquaintance*, however the *content* of what is known, believed, and unknown may differ greatly between social groups and across time. Thus, knowledge is *relative* and varies depending on the social group, both within societies and within the subgroups in those societies. In other words, different societies know different things to be true; they have different social stocks of knowledge or different knowledge of acquaintance.

Schutz referred to a society's culture, norms, and institutions as **life-world structures**—parts of the life-world people use to make sense of their experiences and interactions with others. He argued that many life-world structures are assumed to exist unquestionably and are therefore taken for granted in everyday life. Referring to the elevator example, most people do not think about how to operate an elevator when they enter one; they simply step in, press a button, and arrive at the desired floor. This is because an elevator, and its basic operation, is a life-world structure that exists unquestionably. However, if one stepped into the elevator, pressed a button and nothing happened, the life-world structure would come into question.

Life-world structures come into question when their assumed **validity** (agreed upon logic or correctness) becomes doubtful or when what may have been perceived as reasonable is no longer possible. When life-world structures come into question, individuals analyze the situation given their surroundings and other life-world structures. This analysis continues until a logical and adequate solution is created. According to Schutz, the new solution becomes a new life-world structure with the same unquestionable characteristics of the old life-world structure.

Intersubjectivity

A central component of phenomenology is **intersubjectivity**, a condition in which more than one individual shares a common perception of reality. Despite their belief that human experiences are filtered through each individual's consciousness, phenomenologists note that no individual maintains a unique interpretation of the social world. Instead, individuals live in an intersubjective world, in which many interpret a common world. Intersubjectivity occurs when two or more people interact to construct meanings or "common sense" knowledge. This "common sense" knowledge is then used as a resource to interpret meanings in the life-world. Schutz argued that when people share common sense, they share a definition of a situation. For phenomenologists, understanding the social world cannot occur unless there is an understanding of the intersubjective reality of the people being researched.

Schutz defined two elements of intersubjectivity: we-relationships and they-relationships. He asserted that the beginning point of intersubjectivity is the *we-relationship*. The world of "we" is not private to individuals, but is *our* world, the one common intersubjective world, which is right there in front of us. Face-to-face relationships form the common lived experience of the world in we-relationships. Consequently, the we-relationship is critical to forming social reality and the social world. In the we-relationship, individuals come together with different subjective viewpoints of knowledge and experience. These viewpoints are then shared among the individuals, and together they create a new common subjective reality, which they now share.

Schutz further posited that an essential aspect of intersubjectivity through the we-relationship is mutual understanding. Mutual understanding occurs when an individual imagines the world from another person's perspective. Schutz argued mutual understanding is critical for a true intersubjective understanding of each person's subjective reality. Taken a step further, during an intersubjective interaction, one individual expects to bring about a certain action by another, therefore impacting the other person's action. When an expected response does not happen, the situation may become confusing. For example, when business executives in the United States meet clients for the first time, the encounter usually includes introductions and handshakes. A business executive might say hello and extend a hand for the client to shake. The action of the business executive creates an expectation of the client (a handshake). If the response does not occur, the situation becomes confusing.

In apposition to we-relationships Schutz also defined *they-relationships* in the intersubjective world, that is, relationships between people who are not intimately connected or engaged in we-relationships. In *they-relationships*, people are influenced by others who are distant from them and with whom they do not directly interact. Examples of they-relationships are contemporaries and observers. *Contemporaries* are individuals who co-exist, or live during the same time but who do not enter direct relationships. Schutz asserted that individuals gain knowledge from contemporaries, but from a distance and not through personal contact. An example is the impact famous actors or athletes have on ordinary people's lives. *Observers* are people who observe specific we-relationships. Because they are observing rather than participating, observers can only indirectly interpret the intersubjectivity and motives of the we-relationship. An example of an observer of we-relationships is a social researcher doing ethnographic research. **Ethnographic research** is a form of social research in which the researcher observes people in their natural surroundings to better understand their daily routines, interpersonal interactions, and other elements of social life. By observing individuals in their everyday lives, ethnographic researchers become observers of individuals' we-relationships.

ETHNOMETHODOLOGY

Ethnomethodology, created by Harold Garfinkel (1917–2011), is a theory based on the phenomenological and symbolic interactionist belief that social order is created through individuals' interactions in everyday life. It seeks to understand the methods through which individuals work to create social order by studying the "common-sense" knowledge held by members of society. To clarify, "ethno" means ordinary or everyday and "method" means mechanism. Thus, ethnomethodology is the study of the ordinary or everyday mechanisms individuals use to assemble social life.

Societal Members and the Emergence of Structures

Ethnomethodology was developed to complement more traditional approaches to sociology, particularly structural functionalism, to provide a more comprehensive view of social life. In connection with this, ethnomethodology critiques structural functionalism's view of individuals in society. Garfinkel, for example, argued that structural sociologists viewed human beings as cultural "dopes" who behave in whatever manner society dictates they should behave. Structural theorists did, in fact, believe that broader structural and cultural forces dictate human behavior, and these theories accorded the individual very little *agency* (that is, the ability to act based on free will) because they believed human action is determined by the structure of society. Conversely, Garfinkel viewed individuals in society as knowledgeable beings that actively create meaning and reality through everyday conversations and actions. According to Garfinkel, structures in society are created, negotiated, and maintained by individuals in society. Thus, ethnomethodology views people in society as *members* rather than simply as individuals. The ethnomethodological view of individuals as members emphasizes the role individuals play in creating society and its structures as well as the individuals' membership in that society. Whereas an individual can simply exist, a member must actively work to maintain membership in the group and, by extension, the group itself.

Ethnomethodologists also differ from structural theorists in their views of the different elements that define society. An example is Durkheim's concept of *social facts*. Durkheim argued that social facts are aspects of society such as culture, norms, and values that are external and coercive to individuals. Durkheim argued that individuals have little influence on how social facts are created, maintained, or changed. In contrast, ethnomethodologists argue that social facts are created by members' interpretive work and interactions. From this perspective, society's members work to actively produce social structures. Ethnomethodology therefore is similar to symbolic interactionism, which focuses on the creation of meaning through individual interaction. However, ethnomethodology is different from symbolic interactionism because it goes beyond examining individual interactions and instead focuses more on the methods members in society use to make sense of the world and to create social facts within society. In other words, symbolic interactionism is concerned with *what* social realities, structures, and identities are created through social interaction; ethnomethodologists are interested in *how* those social realities, structures, and identities are produced.

Ethnomethodologists view social structures as *emergent*, or coming into existence after rather than before social action. From an ethnomethodological perspective, social life unfolds as members participate in it. For example, an individual may plan a particular course of action, but whether or not that individual proceeds with the plan will depend on reactions from others, which cannot be known until the action begins. Based on others' reactions, the individual may proceed in a different direction from the one originally intended. Hence, the action unfolds as social life takes place rather than being predetermined.

One way Garfinkel demonstrated the emergence of social structures is through **breaching experiments**, field studies in which a researcher breaks a social norm to observe the reactions of others. If no reaction occurs, Garfinkel argued, the view held by Durkheim and other structural functionalists that norms and other social structures are external and coercive to the individual holds up. However, as Garfinkel's experiments showed, when everyday social order is disrupted, individuals' sense of reality becomes disrupted as well. In many cases, they respond to disruptions by working together to reestablish social order. In order to reestablish social order, they use methods to redefine the situation in a way that makes sense to them and to the social context in which the event took place. Ethnomethodologists interpret such situations as evidence that social order is created and maintained through member reaction. Interestingly, some breaching experiments evoked such extreme emotions that the experiments had to be stopped. Ethnomethodologists argue that such an extreme reaction demonstrates how important it is for members of society to maintain a sense of social order. In other breaching experiments, the sociologist involved was actually able to get the participants to adhere to a new social norm, again reinforcing the notion that social norms emerge through members' actions.

Ethnomethodologists also view society and its members in terms of accomplishment. Specifically, ethnomethodologists examine the methods through which members of society accomplish "common sense" social categories. Other theories view social categories as ascribed. To distinguish between these viewpoints, to *accomplish* means to carry out or achieve something successfully whereas *ascribe* refers to characteristics one is born with and does not have to put forth effort to achieve. An example of an ethnomethodological accomplishment is Garfinkel's study on gender, which other theorists assert is an ascribed characteristic. The subject of this study was Agnes, an individual who appeared to be a woman in physical appearance and social interaction. Agnes however was anatomically male and thus worked to "accomplish" being a woman in everyday interactions. Garfinkel examined the methods Agnes used to "pass" as a woman in everyday life, how she accomplished "common-sense" routine activities to be viewed as a woman in society. This study, Garfinkel argued, showed how members of society work to accomplish many aspects of the social world that otherwise appear "natural" or ascribed.

Conversation Analysis

Ethnomethodologists also study communication between individuals through a process referred to as *conversation analysis*. Conversation analysis shows how language and talk are the primary method through which local realities are accomplished. In conducting conversation analysis, ethnomethodologists examine everyday conversations to expose the ways individuals organize conversations for them to make sense to all members. One theme in conversational analysis is turn-taking. Ethnomethodologists observe individuals take turns

Doing Gender

Candace West and Don Zimmerman used an ethnomethodological approach to argue gender is created and reproduced through everyday social interactions. They argued that as individuals go about their everyday lives, they assign each other into sex categories, or guess whether each person is male or female. Then they evaluate each others' actions based on how much individuals conform to expected actions within the assigned sex category. At the same time, individuals themselves behave in ways to manage others' interpretations of their genders. As individuals "do gender" in ways that conform to the expectations associated with their sex category, they legitimize gendered stereotypes and expectations by making such differences appear normal and natural. For example, if we expect women to be nurturing to children, and we commonly observe women nurturing children, then it appears natural for women to be nurturing. West and Zimmerman argued that because our expectations for gendered behavior are reproduced in everyday life, individuals can transform gender expectations by doing gender differently. We can see such a transformation taking place as more and more men are involved in childrearing. As we observe more men nurturing children in everyday life, it appears more natural for men to be nurturing. Thus, from an ethnomethodological perspective, gender is an ongoing accomplishment that arises out of everyday situations, and this accomplishment in everyday life reinforces the structural arrangements that make it a significant category in the first place.

Ethnomethodologists believe individuals "socially accomplish" gender through styles of clothing, accessories and mannerisms.

in conversation to develop common-sense knowledge and order. Turn-taking is important because during each turn, knowledge is created and builds upon what was previously said and known. It is through turn-taking conversations that members collectively produce knowledge and a sense of reality.

CRITICAL THEORY

Critical theory is a body of sociological theory that expresses concern over social changes associated with modernity and the Enlightenment, including capitalism, industrialization, and science. Whereas many classical theorists, particularly Emile Durkheim and Herbert Spencer, viewed these changes as progress, critical theorists view these changes with negativity and pessimism. Critical theorists are concerned that science in particular is part of the broader *ruling apparatus*, the system that creates and maintains domination, rather than a mechanism for *emancipation*, or freedom from rule. Critical theory is similar to conflict theory in that both focus on power and social inequality, and both work toward emancipation. Critical theory differs from conflict theory in that it emphasizes the role of ideas in creating and maintaining inequality.

Critical theory is rooted in the classical works of Karl Marx and Max Weber. Marx critiqued a group called the "Young Hegelians" who, based on the work of philosopher G.W.F. Hegel, believed the progression of society exists in the realm of ideas. Once a Hegelian himself, Marx turned against this philosophy and argued that the emphasis on ideas rather than concrete, practical relations perpetuates inequality. Marx believed oppression was an inherent part of the capitalist system and that within capitalism the proletariat contributes to its own oppression through labor. Marx believed the proletariat would eventually gain awareness of this and then work to change the capitalist system. Weber was also apprehensive about the capitalist system, but his concern focused on *rationalization*, the increasing emphasis on means-end efficiency that coincided with the rise of science and capitalism. Weber was more pessimistic than Marx, predicting that increasing bureaucratic power would lead not to revolution but to an *iron cage* of administrative control. These concerns with capitalism and modernity laid the foundation for critical theory.

Critical theory originated at the Frankfurt School during the 1920s through the works of Max Horkheimer (1895–1973), Theodor Adorno (1903–1969), Erich Fromm (1900–1980), and Herbert Marcuse (1898–1979), who borrowed from earlier Western Marxists such as Georgy Lukacs (1885–1971). Critical theory was further advanced by Antonio Gramsci (1891–1937) and Jurgen Habermas (1929–).

Gyorgy Lukacs

Gyorgy Lukacs sought to clarify and expand Marx's critique of capitalism. Lukacs created the concept of *reification* from Marx's *fetishism of commodities*. Marx argued that the relationship between people under capitalism is a relationship between *commodities*, products of labor that are given value. The commodity comes to be viewed as a thing that has its own intrinsic properties rather than as a product of human labor. This view of the commodity leads to the **fetishism of commodities** in which humans relate to each other through the

Lukacs points out that dollar bills are not intrinsically valuable but become valuable when people use them in exchange for goods. *(Wikipedia)*

commodities as if the objects have intrinsic value, thus overlooking their own role in creating the objects and the meanings attributed to them. For example, the dollar bill does not have intrinsic value other than the value of the paper on which it is printed. However, individuals have agreed to treat the dollar bill as if it has value, and subsequently exchange dollar bills for products. After multiple exchanges involving dollar bills, individuals often come to view the dollar bill as valuable in its own right, overlooking the fact that its value exists only because humans attribute value to it.

Marx's concept of the fetishism of commodities suggests this perception of intrinsic value applies to consumer products as well. If a generic pair of shoes sells for $20 and a name-brand pair sells for $100, many people assume the name-brand pair is intrinsically more valuable than the generic. Marx, however, pointed out that in a capitalist system, objects are worth whatever people are willing to pay for them. Therefore, the name-brand shoes may have the same intrinsic value as the generic shoes, but the name-brand shoes appear more valuable because people are willing to pay more for them. Thus, value is determined by people rather than the commodity. People then relate to each other based on these assigned values. If a woman wants to purchase a pair of name-brand

Sociology and Music

Theodor Adorno, a critical theorist from the Frankfurt School, was influential in the fields of musical composition and musicology and often applied sociological theory to his work in music. Musicology is the study of the cultural and historical significance of music, including analyses of biographies of composers, time periods in which different styles of music were created, and social groups who listened to different types of music. Adorno believed music and other forms of entertainment are an integral part of society and that they are used by those in power to exert social control. Adorno argued that jazz and other popular music, rather than being creative artistic expression, made art into a commodity. He believed popular music was a product of a growing culture industry, which churned out superficial popular music to encourage the homogenization of society, and that popular music helped appease the masses. Though Adorno's theories about music and society garnered only mild interest and mixed reactions from other musicologists of his day, supporters of his ideas exist even today. These supporters call for the increase of "art music," traditionally classical music, in classrooms for educational purposes and criticize the use of pop music in children's entertainment programs.

Performance by the Philharmonic Orchestra of Jalisco *(Wikipedia)*

shoes, she must first acquire $100 to pay a vendor for those shoes. The woman's relation to the vendor is mediated by the value assigned to the shoes.

Lukacs argued the fetishism of commodities leads to a process of **reification**, in which the view of things as separate from the individuals who create and assign meaning to them is applied to other parts of society, such as politics, government, and media. According to Lukacs, these institutions are actually controlled by the same group of wealthy individuals that control the capitalist economy. Reification helps these individuals maintain power because people view commodities, the economy, politics, and other major social institutions as beyond the control of individual people. More specifically, rather than view the economic market as controlled by individuals, people largely perceive it as impacted by outside forces, such as natural economic laws. For example, when the cost of gasoline suddenly increases, it is explained as part of a "market force" rather than an act precipitated by people in positions of power. When a particular racial group is portrayed in a stereotypical manner on a television show, it is perceived as a "media representation" rather than a portrayal created by individual people who work for a particular television network. Such misrecognition of the market economy and other social institutions as impacted by forces that are outside of human control is reification.

Lukacs believed the role of critical theory was to expose these mechanisms of control to make people aware of the ways they are dominated. He believed this awareness would lead to social revolution. Frankfurt School theorists Horkheimer and Adorno believed awareness alone would not automatically create resistance, and that critical theory should focus not only on uncovering how domination works but also on how best to alleviate it.

Antonio Gramsci

Antonio Gramsci was an Italian critical theorist who based his work on Marx's ideas. Gramsci argued that wealthy capitalists maintain their power by controlling the spread of ideas through government and other institutions, such as education and media. Gramsci suggested the ruling class maintains **hegemony**, ideological control, over the rest of society by controlling the general culture and ideas of the population. In hegemonic control, people willingly submit to practices that benefit the ruling class and hurt themselves because they are manipulated to misunderstand their situations. For example, in capitalism, workers willingly sell their labor to capitalists because they support the belief that individuals should work hard to make a living even though their work benefits the capitalists more than it benefits themselves. Most workers also support the free-market system even though that very system depresses their wages. Gramsci contrasted hegemony with **coercion**, which is compliance through the use of force, often through military or police control. He posited that when a population is controlled through hegemony, coercion is unnecessary.

Jurgen Habermas

Jurgen Habermas, a critical theorist who spent part of his career at the Frankfurt School, conceptualized society as consisting of two parts: a social system and a lifeworld. A *social system* is a broad, overarching set of institutions (including the economy and the state) that operate together to facilitate reproduction of the human species. *Lifeworld*, borrowed from philosopher Husserl and used by phenomenonologists, refers to the realm of social life characterized by interpersonal relationships and communicative action. **Communicative action** is social interactions among two or more people through which mutual understanding is achieved. Habermas argued the social system is increasingly taking over the lifeworld through the erosion of the public sphere, overemphasis of scientific knowledge, and lack of political participation that results from a legitimation crisis.

Habermas posited that the rise of the *public sphere*—forums such as newspapers and cafes in which debate and discussion (communicative action) can take place—facilitated the transformation from feudalism to capitalism by providing a space for the transformation of ideas through communication. Within capitalism, however, the public sphere is being eroded as a result of increasing state intervention in major institutions, such as the economy and ever-expanding bureaucratic structures. Habermas believed this decline of the public sphere inhibits communication between individuals, which leads to increasing state control over social life. The goal of critical theory is to illustrate this process so the public sphere can be resurrected and emancipatory social change can occur.

In line with other critical theorists, Habermas was critical of the role of scientific knowledge in capitalist societies. To explain the problematic role of science, Habermas distinguished between three types of knowledge: (1) empirical/analytic (scientific) knowledge, which focuses on the concrete, material world; (2) hermeneutic/historical knowledge, which focuses on meanings and human history; and (3) critical knowledge, which focuses on power and domination. Each of these knowledge types corresponds to a particular human interest. Empirical/analytic knowledge corresponds to human interest in controlling and manipulating the environment to ensure reproduction of the human species. Hermeneutic/historical knowledge corresponds to human interest in understanding the meanings people attribute to things. Critical knowledge corresponds to human interest in freedom and emancipation.

Habermas argued that capitalist societies increasingly emphasize empirical/analytic knowledge at the expense of other types of knowledge and that such a focus prioritizes technical control over human understanding and freedom. Noting that the social sciences use empirical/analytic knowledge to understand human societies, Habermas argued that because of this focus the social sciences were increasingly becoming a mechanism of social control.

In other words, since the purpose of scientific knowledge is to learn about something in order to control it, and the social sciences are using a scientific approach to understand human populations, then the scientific knowledge generated by the social sciences contributes to the state's ability to control human populations. He proposed that if social scientists wanted to have a different impact on society—such as understanding or freedom rather than control—they had to create or focus on a different form of knowledge, such as hermeneutic or critical.

It was Habermas' belief that scientific knowledge is also problematic because it is increasingly applied to political issues, pointing out that political issues are framed as technical problems rather than issues to be discussed and are being resolved through the scientific calculations of "experts," which contributes to further state and bureaucratic regulation. According to Habermas, this increasing regulation has led to a **legitimation crisis**, a situation in which individuals do not feel sufficiently motivated to participate in the political process. Because political issues are being framed as technical problems, individuals are not engaging in communicative action to resolve them. This legitimation crisis allows for even greater state control, which leads to greater and greater domination of the system over the lifeworld. The consequence is an increasing lack of meaning in the lifeworld.

Habermas suggested a way to resolve the legitimation crisis and the social system's overtaking of the lifeworld is to reinstate communicative action. He believed that critical theorists could use people's frustration over the lack of meaning in the lifeworld to help reinstate the balance between system and lifeworld. Such social change, according to Habermas, would require restoring the public sphere and reinstating communicative action in social life.

SUMMARY
Phenomenology, ethnomethodology, and critical theory extend and expand upon previous theories. Phenomenology and ethnomethodology use some of the principles of symbolic interactionism in their focus on meanings and subjectivity, but they engage in a deeper examination of the roles of consciousness and individual action in creating subjective interpretations and the social world itself. Critical theory builds upon conflict theory in its emphasis on power and inequality, but it deepens the analysis by questioning the role of knowledge in perpetuating unequal power arrangements.

Further Reading

Calhoun, Craig. *Critical Social Theory*. Malden, Mass.: Blackwell Publishers, 1995.
Francis, David, and Stephen Hester. *An Invitation to Ethnomethodology: Language, Society and Social Interaction*. Thousand Oaks, Calif.: Sage, 2004.

Luckmann, Thomas. *Phenomenology and Sociology.* Middlesex, England: Penguin Books, 1978.

Ritzer, George. *Sociological Theory, Eighth Edition.* New York: McGraw-Hill, 2011.

Turner, Jonathan H. *The Structure of Sociological Theory, Seventh Edition.* Belmont, Calif.: Wadsworth, 2003.

CHAPTER 7

POSTRUCTURALIST
AND POSTMODERN THEORIES

The later part of the 20th century gave way to poststructuralist and postmodern theories, which focus on the significance of language, media, and technology in contemporary Western societies. Poststructuralism emphasizes the impact of language as a mechanism of social control. Postmodern theories argue that Western societies have moved beyond the modern era and are characterized by advanced technology, a rejection of science, and blurred boundaries between previously distinguishable phenomena. In line with postmodernism, the next development in sociological theory is synthesis, which seeks to combine the main ideas of previously incompatible theories.

MICHEL FOUCAULT

Michel Foucault (1926–1984) is associated with several schools of thought, including structuralism, poststructuralism, and postmodernism, but Foucault rejected the classification of his work with any particular theoretical paradigm. Instead he focused on the history of knowledge and its relation to social control, human sexuality, and social institutions, such as medicine, psychiatry, and criminal justice.

Epistemes

Foucault's early work focused on the history of knowledge. Foucault perceived knowledge as a social phenomenon, existing within a certain time and place, but not necessarily arising from individuals. He conceptualized knowledge as an unconscious, collective structure unique to each historical time period. In any given era, Foucault believed, there is an underlying and accepted set of knowledge and beliefs that define the social behavior of the time. Foucault called this set of knowledge the **episteme**. The episteme is part of the structure of the society, which exists outside of the individuals within that society. In this sense, individuals are born into a particular episteme, which exists separate from them but structures their thoughts. As individuals learn the knowledge of their society, they learn to think within the episteme of their particular socio-historical moment. Foucault suggested that people are confined by the episteme in which they live. They are unable to think outside this episteme, but because it is unconscious, they are not even aware of it.

Foucault's concept of the episteme may contradict the ways we typically think about knowledge. Individuals often believe their thoughts are their own private inventions and that they are free to think whatever they want. Foucault's theory contradicts this belief and posits that individuals' thoughts are shaped by the society they live in. In Foucault's later work, he incorporated the concept of power into this scheme. He argued that society (specifically the state or dominant governing body) exerts control over individuals by shaping the thoughts and ideas people are able to have. For example, if people believe sitting in their seat during a math class is normal and doing jumping jacks is deviant, most will select to sit in their seats. They probably view their choice as an act of free will, a rational choice. Foucault, however, would view this action as resulting from state control, as agents of the state determined jumping jacks during class were deviant, created consequences for such actions, and convinced society's members to define jumping jacks the same way. As a result of state definitions, individuals may follow a rule even if it is not in their best interest. Although the individuals may benefit more from doing jumping jacks than from sitting, sitting benefits the state because it contributes to social order.

Discursive Formation
Foucault analyzed the process through which new concepts are developed, arguing that concepts are created through **discourse**, formal discussions and writings about a topic. Each discipline has its own discourse, such as medical discourse, scientific discourse, legal discourse, and so on. He called the process of creating concepts through discourse **discursive formation** and explained that concepts created through discursive formation helped define and frame the world around us. Foucault used psychiatry to demonstrate the process of discursive formation. He argued that the term "mental illness" is a concept that was created through discursive formation within modern psychiatry. Before psychiatry, insanity and mental illnesses were collectively called "madness." Through the discourse of psychiatry different types of mental illnesses that were previously grouped together came to be defined as separate illnesses, such as

depression, obsessive-compulsive disorder, and schizophrenia. Madness cannot be treated, but once it was established that there were different types of madness, it became possible to talk about and develop treatments for these distinct illnesses. Foucault emphasized that not anyone can define objects within a certain discourse. Instead, there are specific rules about who can create and identify objects within a discourse, and there is a strict set of procedures that must be followed in doing so. For example, only those who have been professionally trained and certified as psychiatrists can diagnose and define mental illnesses.

Foucault argued that discursive formation is important because it is the process through which concepts are developed. Once a concept is developed, the thing the concept represents exists. Thus, it is through discursive formation that objects are created. This is particularly significant when the objects created are different types of people. In psychiatry, for example, before the concept "schizophrenia" was created there were no schizophrenics. Once the concept was created through discursive formation, then certain people could be singled out and identified as "schizophrenic."

Michel Foucault, 1926–1984

Michel Foucault was born in Poitiers, France, on October 15, 1926. Though his father hoped Michel would follow in his footsteps and become a surgeon, the younger Foucault was more interested in the humanities. Foucault attended the prestigious Ecole Normal Superieure graduate school with hopes of becoming an academic. While in graduate school, he became deeply depressed and began seeing a psychiatrist. This prompted a fervent interest in psychology, and Foucault went on to earn degrees in psychology and philosophy in 1952. He began teaching psychology, but was unhappy teaching and decided to leave France for a time. Returning to France in 1960, Foucault enrolled at the University of Clermont-Ferrand to complete a doctorate in philosophy. While working on his doctorate, Foucault met another philosopher, Daniel Defert, with whom he developed a deep bond, eventually entering into a relationship that was to last for more than twenty years. During the years following his meeting Defert, Foucault published some of his famous works, including *The Order of Things*, *The Archaeology of Knowledge*, and *Discipline and Punish: the Birth of the Prison*. In the late 1970s, Foucault came under criticism because some of his new work partially contradicted previous works. Foucault dismissed these criticisms, saying that the purpose of life and work is to become someone that you were not in the beginning. Foucault died from AIDS on June 24, 1986, at the age of 57. Following his death, Defert founded the first AIDS-awareness organization in France in Foucault's memory.

Discursive formation involves not only the creation of objects but also a set of prescribed behaviors regarding what to do with them. Thus, once an individual is identified as "schizophrenic," there are certain therapies and treatments psychiatrists are expected to prescribe to treat the condition.

Discipline and Punish

Foucault analyzed the criminal justice system in his book *Discipline and Punish: The Birth of the Prison*. This book opens with a brief history of criminal punishment in France, comparing the visible forms of punishment such as public torture and execution, which were common in the preindustrial era, with the private confinement of prisoners in the modern era. Foucault argued this transformation in the treatment of criminals was related to the rise of human sciences, including psychology, scientific medicine, and social work. These sciences allowed for a new understanding of the human subject as a being that could be understood in scientific terms. Science created new criteria by which individuals could be observed, measured, and evaluated to determine the extent to which they are "normal." The human sciences also created an understanding of the human subject as malleable, something that could be shaped, changed, or molded through certain disciplinary techniques.

Foucault argued that this new understanding of the human subject facilitated the growth of a new form of punishment. Rather than simply punish the body, as in premodern times, the new form sought to punish the soul. In prison, the criminal is subject to solitude and boredom, and the only thing to do is reflect and feel remorse for the crime. The purpose for detaining a criminal in prison is rehabilitation, which eventually leads to reentry into society. The idea that individuals can be rehabilitated through certain programs and training is the basis of modern psychiatry. The institutions of law and psychology often work together, as a psychologist may make recommendations to a judge regarding whether or not an inmate is ready to return to society. Thus, the view of the human subject as capable of rehabilitation precipitated a new form of punishing human subjects, and social science and the criminal justice system became interconnected through ideas and discourse.

Although the soul is the target of punishment in the modern era, Foucault argued, the body is not exempt from punishment and in fact plays a critical role. The physical torture of earlier times has been replaced by limiting a prisoner's bodily movement and activity. Someone besides the prisoner decides this, and therefore, even though physical punishment is no longer carried out, the body is still an instrument of control. Prisoners are told when to wake, eat, work, learn, and even relax.

Foucault asserted that the prison system could be viewed as a metaphor for the operation of power throughout society. Regarding the treatment of the body, Foucault contended humans are molded from birth into **docile bodies**, objects that can be used and shaped by those in positions of authority. Foucault used the example of a solider to explain a docile body, explaining that any individual could be transformed into a solider through training and discipline. The key concept here is that soldiers must gain physical strength and endurance; this happens because their bodies are controlled and manipulated by someone else.

Foucault suggested that society disciplines its members through bodily control in several ways. The first of these is *enclosure*. For example, people are enclosed in colleges, monasteries, the military, or factories. This keeps them contained, but it also keeps them controllable—they are, for example, given schedules to follow or information that must be read or listened to. A second way society controls individuals' bodies is through *partitioning*, which discourages groups and breaks them up when they occur. Assigning each person his or her own place, such as a cubicle or school desk, can help prevent alliances among individuals, making them easier to control. A third way individuals' bodies are controlled is through *functional sites*, which act as a sort of gate. For example, a port is a functional site that can control the influx and outflow of goods, diseases, and importantly, ideas. Another feature of functioning sites is that they are built to accommodate overseeing and partitioning. For example, a factory may be designed to allow a supervisor to walk up and down long aisles

Desks in a classroom can be used to partition students, keeping them separate from each other and easily observed by the teacher. *(Wikipedia)*

between tables of workers. This places the workers at a safe distance apart and allows the supervisor to observe all of them individually while at the same time comparing their work. In contrast, if a factory were designed with small round tables, workers could easily talk and conspire amongst themselves without being detected, and it would be more difficult to check their work. Finally, Foucault discussed the function of *time tables*, which serve to force individuals to do certain things at certain times. Like criminals in a prison, children in school are told when to wake, eat, work, learn, and play. Punishments for being late or not adhering to the schedule can be severe. Not only are there punishments such as detention, but failing to keep up with the schedule can create a perpetual cycle; a student who is late for a lesson may miss an assignment, which will have to be completed perhaps at the expense of another scheduled activity or assignment, putting the student still further behind. The overwhelming build-up is incentive to keep students on track. Such examples demonstrate ways society controls its members by controlling their bodies, even while people may believe they are free.

The History of Sexuality
Foucault's final work was a set of volumes concerning the history and discursive formation of sexuality. Foucault noted that many ideas and opinions about sexuality in his time were influenced by the **repressive hypothesis**, the belief that many societies have sought to repress natural human sex drives. This hypothesis holds that sex is often a taboo subject, and discussion about it is discouraged and repressed. Foucault challenged this hypothesis. He maintained that in an effort to create socially acceptable ways to talk about sex, there was in fact an increase in sexual discourse. Foucault argued that there has never been a restriction on speaking about sex; rather, there has been a change in the way in which sex can be spoken about. For example, Western societies with strong Judeo-Christian traditions historically defined sex as either moral or sinful. Over time, with the rise of scientific medicine, sexual discourse became more medical in nature, and sex was defined as either normal or pathological. Foucault noted this change was really only a substitution; *normal* had replaced *morally right*, and *pathological* had replaced *sinful* without any real change in meaning. In other words, what had changed was not people's views of sexuality but sexual discourse.

POSTMODERN THEORY
Postmodern theory is a branch of contemporary sociological theory with two main characteristics. First, postmodern theory rejects the idea of an objective truth. Instead, postmodern thinkers believe truth is *relative*—it varies depending on the knower and is subject to human perception. In other words, postmodern theorists believe there is not just one, concrete, absolute truth "out

there" waiting to be discovered. Extending this idea, even if there were one absolute truth, it is not possible for humans to know which truth is the "real" truth, so that real truth is not relevant for human life. Instead, what is relevant is what people *believe* is true. Secondly, postmodern theory rejects the idea of a **metanarrative**, a common and comprehensive account of history or knowledge. A metanarrative can be thought of as a story about a story. For example, the actual timeline of historical events would be a narrative, but a history textbook retelling that story in a uniform fashion to all students across public schools in America would be considered a metanarrative. Because the metanarrative may or may not be an accurate reflection of the actual timeline, postmodern thinkers argue people in contemporary Western societies have lost faith in metanarratives.

Jean-Francois Lyotard

Jean-Francois Lyotard (1924–1998) was especially critical of the idea of meta-narratives, whether they dealt with history or scientific knowledge. Throughout history, for example, individuals have sought knowledge in part for the purpose of scientific advancement. As scientific knowledge advances and is supported by research, it becomes generally accepted. There may be controversy as previous metanarratives are exchanged for new ones, but the scientific process has historically prevailed. It was in this way that societies moved from believing the Earth is flat to knowing that it is round.

In his criticism of metanarratives, Lyotard argued that in contemporary society knowledge is no longer an end in itself but a commodity that is produced and consumed. Whereas in the past advanced scientific knowledge and training were available to only a few members of society, the spread and development of communication and technology has made knowledge more accessible to the general population. For example, only a few decades ago, all research was done in person in libraries or laboratories. Today, few students ever need to set foot in a library because they can easily access e-books and articles via the Internet. While this has made knowledge easier to obtain, it has at the same time made it much more difficult to determine what is real or not real or what is true or not true, as the ease of manipulating information has also increased. Consider pictures altered with Photoshop, a program readily available to the general population. As photo-editing programs improve, what we see may not be real at all, except as an image created by someone. The same is true of information available on the Internet; it is very easily created, manipulated, or changed in such a way that is misleading or entirely untrue.

Lyotard argued that knowledge is increasingly produced by those in power and distributed selectively to the population. For example, media outlets such as news stations are often owned by corporations, which often have a political agenda. Lyotard predicted that in the future, nations will fight over the control of information instead of over territories or natural resources. This prediction has in fact begun to take place, as evidenced by recent battles between China and Google over what information should be available to Chinese citizens via the Internet. With governments and other powerful entities able to decide what information is distributed, it becomes difficult or impossible to know what information to trust. As a result, Lyotard suggested, society has lost faith in knowledge, and no longer believes in scientific knowledge as a metanarrative.

Lyotard further explained that this loss of faith in metanarratives has led to a problem with **legitimation**, the process by which an authority figure earns the right to have authority in a certain area. For example, in the United States, a person does not have the authority to sign a bill into law until American citizens legitimize that person by electing him or her to the presidency. Similarly, a person does not have the authority to treat a medical condition until he or she is legitimized by completing several years of medical school training. It would be impossible for every citizen to be an expert on every topic, so societies collectively agree upon a set of expectations for the role of U.S. President, a medical professional, or any other social role. This way, a person who embodies a certain societal role can be expected to have certain knowledge and skill sets, and we collectively agree to trust those roles. However, Lyotard explained, as people lose faith in knowledge it becomes more difficult to trust the people spreading that knowledge. For example, in the past, citizens trusted newscasters to provide them with an accurate account of current events. Today, however, there are a variety of television news sources that often provided widely different accounts of the same events. Because the information about one thing or one event is so different, Lyotard would argue the general public may lose faith in the role of the newscaster as a result of these different accounts.

Jean Baudrillard

Jean Baudrillard (1929–2007) is another postmodern theorist who was particularly interested in symbols and social meanings. He believed consumption and consumerism drive Western societies, but not simply the consumption of material goods. Though we consume material goods on the surface, Baudrillard argued we are really consuming the *meanings* of those material goods. Baudrillard explained there are only so many goods people actually need. To get people to continue to buy more things, they must be convinced that they need them, which Baudrillard argued is done through advertising, where material goods are assigned meanings that make them appear more desirable. For example, we might need to buy clothing to keep warm, but advertising encourages us to buy clothes with a particular brand name because we are attracted to the meaning the brand name suggests—that people who wear things with the brand name are wealthy or popular. Baudrillard further argued that such advertised mean-

The Matrix

Many people have suggested the popular movie *The Matrix* is based on Baudrillard's ideas about simulacra and simulation. In the film, humanity has been enslaved by intelligent machines that use humans as an energy source. Humans live in pods, with their brains connected to machines. The world as we know it is revealed to be a computer program that is delivered directly to the humans' brains. A few humans have realized that the world they "live" in is actually a false reality, and are able to unhook themselves from the pods and form a resistance against the machines in the real world, which is called Zion. This storyline has a clear connection to Baudrillard's concept of simulation and simulacra. A copy of Baudrillard's book, *Simulacra and Simulation*, even makes a cameo appearance in the film, and directors of the film required all the actors to read the book. However, when interviewed about *The Matrix*, Baudrillard himself said the movie misinterpreted his theories. The humans "living" in the computer-programmed false reality were essentially dreaming. This is not a simulation but simply an illusion. Baudrillard explained that humans in *The Matrix* were either in the reality of Zion or in the illusion of the Matrix. *The Matrix* is therefore not a simulation of reality; a simulation of reality would look like Zion. In contrast, in our society, there is no Zion, because there is no reality at all, only the simulation of reality. Therefore, according to Baudrillard, *The Matrix* takes his concept of simulation to a literal and extreme level, distorting his intent. Though it may not be a true representation of Baudrillard's work, *The Matrix* raises several interesting questions about the nature of reality and opens the door for thought-provoking discussion about Baudrillard's concepts of simulacra and simulation.

ings are false and can actually serve to confuse us. In other words, advertisements make us think we need certain goods or that certain goods will make us happy, so we spend time (and money) trying to acquire them. However, Baudrillard pointed out, what we buy in this manner does not provide the promised happiness or satisfaction and so we continue to seek more products, believing they will provide us with happiness or satisfaction while our true needs are obscured in the process.

To support his conclusions, Baudrillard analyzed different types of values objects have. He explained some need is automatically embedded in the products we consume in the form of utility, or *use value*, as originally explained by Karl Marx. The use value of a pair of sneakers would be to protect our feet. Marx also noted objects have *exchange value*, or the amount of money one could get when selling the object. Baudrillard believed there are two other types of needs assigned to objects through advertising to keep people buying more goods.

One of these needs is called **sign value**, which is the meaning of an object in relation to other objects. All bracelets, for example, serve the same function of decorating a wrist, but a gold bracelet might signify, or have a sign value, that the wearer is in a certain social class, while a rubber bracelet might signify that the wearer supports a certain cause. Though the use value of both is the same, the sign value varies considerably. The other type of need Baudrillard proposed is called **symbolic value**, which is the meaning a person or society assigns an object, or what it symbolizes. A diamond ring, for example, serves the same function as all other rings but symbolizes, or has a symbolic value, that the wearer is engaged to be married. Baudrillard believed individuals are taught sign and symbolic values through advertisements. Convinced that we need not just to protect our feet or decorate our wrists, but that we need to signify our place in society and symbolize our status, we consume more products. These products are then quickly replaced with the next product that we are also convinced we need. According to Baudrillard, sign values and symbolic values mask the use value of objects and leave us with a false sense of reality.

In an extreme example of postmodern thought, Baudrillard later theorized that reality does not exist at all. He argued humans have replaced reality with symbols and signs. Rather than living in reality we are living in a **simulation** of reality. Baudrillard uses the example of an ill person to demonstrate what he means by simulation. A person might *fake* an illness by lying in bed and not going to school. However, a person who *simulates* an illness will actually generate symptoms of the illness. This individual might shiver, express little interest in eating, and/or become weak and lethargic. Baudrillard explained that the faker can easily be discovered because reality is only being masked. The simulator, however, blurs the line between real and imaginary. The simulator produces real symptoms, so an outside observer cannot know if he or she is, in reality, sick or not. Baudrillard then pointed out that if any symptom can be simulated, then any illness could be real or not real, and reality loses its meaning. Baudrillard called these replications of reality, such as the symptoms of an illness, **simulacra**. Through the use of simulacra, according to Baudrillard, all of reality is simulated.

Baudrillard believed all of contemporary society is replaced with simulacra and is being simulated. He explained that there are four stages in the development of simulacra. In the first stage, reality is reflected. This is a true representation of reality. An example of this would be an objective newspaper account of an event. In the second stage, reality is masked or perverted. This could be an opinionated blogger who writes only about one side of the event. In the third stage, the *absence* of reality is masked. On a day when few interesting events occur, news outlets might overhype an insignificant story to fill airtime. Finally, reality is forgone altogether. Urban myths and old wives tales are examples of this fourth stage, as they are so widespread as to become common knowledge, even though they may not be true. Soon, it becomes difficult to determine what is real and what is not. Baudrillard contended that in the United States and Western Europe all aspects of society have now reached this fourth stage and that we are living in a simulation of reality, unable to know what true reality is. All objects have been replaced with sign values and symbolic values and are therefore simulacra instead of reality.

SYNTHESIS

There are a wide variety of ideas and paradigms within the body of sociological theory, many of which are contradictory. While each school of thought has different followers and proponents, they all have value to the field of sociology. Some theorists have attempted to combine elements from several theories into a new, unified theory in a process called **synthesis**. Synthesis strives to find similarities between opposing theories in attempt to reconcile them or find a middle ground.

Anthony Giddens

Anthony Giddens (1938–) created a synthesis theory that combines micro- and macro-level analyses. In microsociology, emphasis is placed on the actions and behaviors of individual members or smaller units of society. Individuals are considered active *agents*, meaning they have *agency* or power to act based on free will and personal choice. In macrosociology, emphasis is placed on broad social institutions or social structure. Giddens rejected the idea that either of these methods of analysis was correct on its own. He argued that agency and structure are inseparably connected in a **duality of structure**. Giddens believed it would be impossible for either agency or structure to exist without the presence of the other.

The evolution of language and symbols is an example of the duality of structure in action. Agents create language and symbols in order to understand each other. For example, the visible spectrum of light existed before language did, but it was only when different colors became classified and labeled that their meaning could be conveyed between agents. Once colors were identified, a person could say "pink" and be confident that the person hearing the word would be envisioning the same color. Over time, the color pink has come to signify different things, and those significations have become part of the structure of society, which in turn influences the behavior of agents. In contemporary U.S. society, for example, the color pink is associated with baby girls; blue is associated with baby boys. People act differently toward baby girls and baby boys; the pink or blue outfits, each with its respective signification, can influence this behavior. Some people may even get confused around a baby dressed in yellow or another gender-neutral color. Ironically, the pink and blue of contemporary U.S. culture is a relative novelty. Historically, baby boys were dressed in pink, which was considered a watered-down version of the masculine color red, and baby girls were dressed in blue, the color worn by the Virgin Mary. It was not until a few decades ago that these preferences were reversed. This progression is an example of agents and structure interacting with and influencing each other. Agents defined pink and its meanings, which became a part of structure, which impacts the behavior of agents.

Because agents and structure continually shape each other, Giddens argued they exist in a double hermeneutic relationship. **Hermeneutics** means the process of understanding or interpreting something. A **double hermeneutic** involves a relationship between who is seeking to understand and what is being understood; it is the process of understanding something that in turn influences that understanding or interpretation.

In physical science, single hermeneutics are used. Scientists might seek to understand the laws of physics, for example, but the process is a one-way street because the laws of physics are not affected by being studied. They do not change based on our understanding, nor do scientists or humanity change based on what is discovered. But social science, Giddens explained, uses double hermeneutics because, unlike the laws of physics, people and society *are* affected by being studied. As social scientists make observations and findings about society, these findings become part of society and change the way people think and act. Therefore, social science findings both affect society and are affected by society, creating a two-way street of understanding.

Pierre Bourdieu

Pierre Bourdieu (1930–2002) is another theorist who practiced synthesis. Like Giddens, Bourdieu rejected the idea of sharp contradictions in sociology, such as macro versus micro or conflict theory versus functionalism. However, Bourdieu did focus on the conflict between subjectivism and objectivism. *Subjectivists* emphasize the importance of individual experiences and interpretations of those experiences by agents. *Objectivists* believe reality is independent of human consciousness and that it does not change because of agents' interpretations. Stated differently, objectivists believe there is a single, objective reality out there waiting to be discovered whereas subjectivists believe that what is significant to sociology is what people hold to be their reality. Bourdieu felt both of these positions were too extreme, arguing that subjectivity and objectivity interact with each other and should not be viewed separately.

Bourdieu believed every individual is characterized by a certain set of objective conditions, for example being male or middle class, but that the same individual will also engage in unique, subjective experiences because no two people have exactly the same life. These individual experiences will be influenced by objective conditions. For example, many women experience childbirth, but the experience is different for a middle-class woman in the 21st century than it was for a peasant-class woman in the 17th century. As individuals live out their subjective experiences under objective conditions, they develop a set of perceptions, dispositions, and tastes called a **habitus**. The habitus dictates the thoughts and behaviors of an individual yet is so internalized that an individual is not even consciously aware of it.

Subjective experiences will be different for people with different objective conditions, but they can also be similar for people with similar objective conditions. Kindergarten is a very different experience for a middle-class student living in a suburb and for a working-class student living in an urban center. But it is probably very similar for two middle-class students who live in the suburbs. Those two students, and other students like them, are likely to grow to share common dispositions and preferences, or have a similar habitus. Bourdieu believed members of the same social class often share a similar habitus as a result of their similar life experiences. This shared habitus is passed on to each new generation, providing a common experience for all members of the social class.

Bourdieu analyzed the socialization of young members of groups into a shared habitus, which allows class divisions to be perpetuated. This distinct socialization is most clearly seen in the aesthetic preferences of the members of different classes. Bourdieu believed that taste in things such as food, clothing, music, and even furniture is internalized by children at an early age and helps to maintain class divisions. If a person encounters someone with similar aesthetic tastes, it is a reasonable assumption that it is someone who belongs to the same social class. Likewise, it is reasonable for people to assume that someone with different tastes belongs to a different class.

It is on the basis of such evidence that Bourdieu determined that economic capital is not the only feature that distinguishes social classes. In connection with this, Bourdieu posited that social class is a combination of economic capital, social capital, cultural capital, and symbolic capital that distance members of one class from another. **Social capital** is advantage gained from the people one knows; it is a network of connections and relationships. **Cultural capital** refers to knowledge that is highly valued in a society, such as worldliness, knowing many languages, or being well versed in art or literature. **Symbolic capital** is another way of saying honor or prestige. Being president of an organization or being a famous athlete are examples of symbolic capital. The four types of capital interact with and contribute to each other. For example, social capital could help an individual get a job, which secures economic capital, and economic capital allows a person to go to a prestigious school, which provides cultural, social, and symbolic capitals.

The combination of habitus and capital help define what social groups an individual belongs to, and by extension, how that person will think and act in a given situation. However, this would be meaningless without a realm in which the individual can act—society. Bourdieu envisioned society as being made up of many **fields**, structured social environments that overlap and interact. Some examples of fields include law, education, arts, and politics. Agents

Self-identity in the Information Age

Anthony Giddens analyzed self-identity in today's technology-driven Information Age. Giddens argued that in the past, self-identity was often handed to people in the form of traditional social roles. For example, many surnames were used to identify the family trade, which was often passed down through multiple generations. Baker, Gardner, Ward, Cooper (a barrel maker), and Day (a dairy farmer) are a small number of the many examples of this practice. Even more recently, self-identity was closely linked to social roles. For example, many American women in 20th century had only one choice of identity—housewife—because a woman's identity was tied to home and husband. Today, however, social roles rarely come with an identity tag. People must therefore create their own self-identity. Giddens believed this freedom to choose one's self-identity is both liberating and frightening because people might be confused about how they should act and who they should be. With the onset of the Internet and social networking sites, the freedom associated with self-identity has increased exponentially. Many people today are almost limitless in their ability to invent an identity of their choosing by presenting whatever information they choose to share through online profiles. This supports Giddens' belief that self-identity does not stem from behavior but from a continued narrative presented by a person. The Internet makes it easier for people to sustain their chosen narratives; at the same time, it allows them to explore and account for their own traits. For example, instead of seeking professional diagnosis, many people have used the Internet as a source of information to diagnose themselves with physical

exercise their habitus and capitals to navigate society and earn social positions in a field. Bourdieu likened this to playing a game. Throughout their lives, agents struggle to either change or maintain their positions in the field, competing over its boundaries. Just as the habitus would be useless without a field on which to exercise it, fields would be static, empty spaces without agents using their habitus to navigate them. Habitus and field, like agency and structure, would each be unable to exist without the other.

SUMMARY

Poststructuralist and postmodern theories challenge the ideas of previous theories about power and social life. Poststructuralists see power embedded in language and discourse, exerting control over individuals for the purpose of social order to benefit the government. This view of power counters the view of conflict theorists, who see power in the hands of a small group of people who benefit from the power arrangements. Postmodern theories contend that changes in

illnesses and even social disorders. With a larger pool of information to draw from, people are increasingly able to construct novel combinations to make up a self-identity.

Many college students today use the Internet to define their identities. *(Wikipedia)*

the economy and technology have led to a situation in which a concrete reality no longer exists, as it is indistinguishable from the simulated realities we experience through screens. Synthesists work within the main sociological paradigms, attempting to integrate theories previously viewed as incompatible.

Further Reading

Best, Steven, and Douglas. Kellner. *Postmodern Theory: Critical Interrogations.* New York: The Guilford Press, 1991.

Cuff, E. C., W. W. Sharrock, and D. W. Francis. *Perspectives in Sociology,* 5th ed. London: Routledge, 2006.

Rabinow, Paul. *The Foucault Reader.* New York: Pantheon Books, 1984.

Ritzer, George. *Sociological Theory,* 8th ed. New York: McGraw-Hill, 2011.

Turner, Jonathan H. *The Structure of Sociological Theory,* 7th ed. Belmont, Calif.: Wadsworth, 2003.

CHAPTER 8

FEMINIST THEORIES

Theories of emancipation are consistent with earlier works of Karl Marx and other conflict and critical theorists, which sought to create a sociology that advocates equal rights for all. Theory designed for the purpose of social change is referred to as **praxis**. Praxis differs from some theories (such as structural functionalism and symbolic interactionism) that seek only to describe society and not affect it. Emancipatory sociologists argue that all knowledge is political, so a sociology that seeks to simply understand but not change society supports society's current arrangements. Emancipatory sociologists argue the question is not whether or not sociology should be political, but what kind of politics sociology wants to support. Key categories in emancipatory sociology are feminist theories, theories of race and ethnicity, postcolonialism, queer theory, and nonhuman theories. Because feminist theory has a longer history than the others cited here, we dedicate the current chapter to feminist theories and summarize the other emancipatory theories in the following chapter.

FEMINIST THEORIES
Feminist theory is based on the observation that women are unequal to men in societies throughout the world. Different feminist theories provide different explanations for why **patriarchy**—male domination over women—exists and how best to eliminate it. Like all social theories, each feminist theory is partly a product of the social and political climate in which it was created. Feminist thought may be divided historically into three waves that parallel the

Women's Movement in the United States and Western Europe. The first wave began in the mid-1700s and continued through the mid-1900s. Liberal and Marxist feminism emerged during this wave. The second wave occurred in the 1960s and 1970s and coincided with the Civil Rights movement in the United States. Radical feminism emerged during this wave. Theories from the first and second waves were mostly written by white, Western women. Third wave feminism, which emerged in the late 1980s, is largely a critique of race, class, and national biases in the first two waves. Third wave theories include intersectional feminism, womanism, and indigenous feminism, which are not only theories of gender emancipation but also advocate emancipation from racism, classism, and colonialism.

Liberal Feminism

Liberal feminist theory, which includes the works of Mary Wollstonecraft, Susan B. Anthony, Elizabeth Cady Stanton, Betty Friedan, and Judith Lorber, among others, focuses on the elimination of sexism in society by giving

Liberal Feminist Activism

Mary Wollstonecraft is credited as writing the first feminist book. Published in 1792, *A Vindication of the Rights of Woman* presented Wollstonecraft's conviction that women were capable of participating in social activities traditionally reserved for men, such as working outside the home, obtaining an education, and participating in politics. She argued that women should not be restricted to the roles of wife and mother but should have opportunities to pursue whatever roles they chose. A few decades after Wollstonecraft's book was published, there was the historic gathering in Seneca Falls, New York, which was organized and attended by prominent first-wave feminists, such as Susan B. Anthony and Elizabeth Cady Stanton. Held in 1848, it was the first meeting in which women had a public platform to discuss policy reforms such as women's right to vote, welfare, marriage, divorce, and child custody.

In addition to advocating for women's rights, Anthony and Stanton were both active in the abolitionist movement that sought to end slavery. A few years after the historical gathering at Seneca Falls, another abolitionist and liberal feminist named Sojourner Truth gave a historic speech that echoed their views from the perspective of a black woman. Titled "Ain't I a Woman?" Truth's speech declared that although she was a woman, her "womanhood" and "femaleness" had never interfered with her ability to do the labor-intensive work men did while also having thirteen children, most of whom were sold into slavery. Truth, like other liberal feminists argued that women were physically capable of doing the women the same opportunities as men. Liberal feminists argue that women have the capability of doing what men do (for example, get an education, hold down jobs, and participate in politics) but contend that women have been denied these opportunities. In connection with this, liberal feminists focus on women's *autonomy* (personal decision making) to argue that women should have the right to choose whether or not to vote, work, or go to school. The primary objective of liberal feminism is to promote and ensure equal rights for women in all aspects of society based on a belief in equal human ability across the sexes.

Liberal feminism was central in the fight for women's *suffrage* (right to vote), which was granted when the 19th Amendment to the U.S. Constitution was passed in 1919. Liberal feminism continued to maintain importance during the second wave, as feminists advocated equal rights and opportunities for women in public spheres such as education and the workplace. These feminists fought for opportunities that would allow women to be economically independent through equal competition with men in a free market economy. In this sense,

things men do but were socially barred from participating in such activities. Her status as a black woman exacerbated the social barriers that constrained white women, but the Civil War and its aftermath would bring about a unique and powerful alliance. With the onset of the Civil War, the struggle for women's rights was put on hold as the movement to end slavery grew in numbers and determination. One year following the end of the Civil War, black abolitionists Sojourner Truth and Fredrick Douglas and feminists Cady Stanton and Anthony joined forces and organized the Equal Rights Association at the 1866 National Women's Rights Convention. The association's purpose was to advocate voting rights for all women and black men. In 1919 the 19th Amendment granted women the right to vote—a great victory for the first feminist wave.

Mary Wollstonecraft *(Library of Congress)*

liberal feminists did not critique American values of individualism, the pursuit of wealth, or democratic freedom, but instead argued that these American values should be attainable by men *and* women. Thus, liberal feminists upheld the capitalist economic system while arguing that women should be able to participate in that system as men's equals.

Liberal feminism was the first feminist theory to provide a significant critique of sociology and other fields of study that were historically dominated by men. Part of the liberal feminist objective was for women to attain advanced degrees and enter academia. As more liberal feminists entered the field of sociology, they began to critique some of the classical sociological theories. They argued, for example, against Durkheim's position that inequalities between the sexes were a consequence of nature. Durkheim had argued that women's roles in society as housewives and mothers resulted from their reproductive biology; men, on the other hand, were not hindered by such biological functions and were therefore free to participate in public roles. Countering Durkheim's views, liberal feminist sociologists asserted that sex differences are socially constructed with no basis in "nature."

The assertion that differences between men and women result from society rather than biology begins with the distinction between sex and gender. **Sex** is the biological classification of being male or female and is defined by chromosomes, hormones, and genitalia. **Gender** refers to the social and cultural expectations associated with being male or female, the characteristics associated with masculinity and femininity. Whereas sex is presumed to be rooted in biology, gender is understood as something that originates in society and is perpetuated through social institutions such as school, family, work, media, and religion. Liberal feminist sociologists have long argued that gender inequality in society is caused by gender rather than sex differences. At the core of this argument is the belief that women are physically, biologically, and naturally equal to men but that men and women are socially unequal because society has created separate roles for men and women and then deemed women's roles less significant than men's. Over time, the idea that women are "naturally" suited to perform those activities socially defined as "feminine" is accepted within the society as normal and appropriate, even though the allocation of those activities to women resulted from the social arrangements determined by that society.

Theoretical development of the distinction between sex and gender led to the notion of the *social construction of gender*, the idea that gender is created, negotiated, and maintained through social interaction. This concept suggests gender has no concrete existence of its own but instead emerges through social institutions and ongoing interactions between people. As a social construction, gender is not a reasonable justification for treating individuals unequally.

Marxist Feminism

Marxist feminism, which includes the works of Mariarosa Dalla Costa, Selma James, Teresa Amott, and Lisa Vogel, was based on the classical works of Karl Marx and Friedrich Engels. Marxist feminists argued that women's oppression is rooted in exploitive labor and production practices that are embedded in capitalism. *Exploitive labor* refers to a situation in which an individual or group unfairly takes advantage of the work of another individual or group for personal gain. *Production* refers to the process through which a product, or end result, of work is created. In the traditional Marxist sense, production refers to the creation of goods, such as those produced on an assembly line. Marxist feminists use the concept of production more broadly, in that a product could be a dinner, a clean house, or even a child.

Marxist feminists viewed capitalism as a system of exploitive power relations resulting in women's subordination to men. Within exploitive power relations, the *dominant group* (those with power) controls all the resources and takes advantage of the *subordinate group* (those without power). Members of the subordinate group have limited choices in society. Consequently, the subordinate group engages in exploitive labor, production that benefits the dominant group. Through exploitive labor, the subordinate group helps the dominant group maintain power while reinforcing its own subordination.

Marxist feminists drew upon Engels's work *The Origin of the Family, Private Property, and the State*, which theorized a relationship between capitalism, the emergence of private property, and men's control over women's reproduction. According to Engels, before the rise of private property, men were not particularly concerned with identifying their biological children. In such a society, there was little need for men to control women. However, since the goal of capitalism is to acquire capital, individuals must be able to claim ownership of money and goods, or *private property*. As capitalism grew, men had more incentive to identify their (particularly male) children, since private property was passed down to male offspring. Furthermore, whereas a woman can always be certain of her biological relationship to a child as a result of giving birth, a man cannot be entirely certain if a newborn child is his. The only way to assure a baby is his offspring is to control his female mate's sexuality and reproduction. By confining women to the home and restricting their access to other men, men can be certain of their biological relationship to their children. This system creates male dominance in the form of **patrilineage**—a system in which all property is passed down through men and, consequently, makes women the property of men.

Once private property was established, women's work remained primarily within the home. Before the Industrial Revolution, women's work within the home was considered a significant part of the family's economic production.

However, the Industrial Revolution, which occurred in conjunction with the rise of capitalism, shifted paid work from the home to the public sphere. Marxist feminists argued this is when women's work within the home became particularly exploitive. In industrial capitalism, work that generates money is valued highest. Because work related to reproduction, childrearing, and housekeeping do not generate money, these forms of production came to be devalued in capitalist societies. Because women did the majority of this work, women became devalued as well. Marxist feminists contended women's work within the home was *exploitive labor* because it was unpaid and undervalued while being essential for capitalism.

Whereas liberal feminists argued women should be allowed to enter the paid workforce, Marxist feminists argued that the consequence of women working in the paid workforce was that women were now expected to do two jobs: their paid work outside the home and their unpaid work inside the home. This phenomenon, in which a woman completes the majority of housework and childcare after working a full day in the paid labor sphere, was referred to as the **second shift**.

Marxist feminists proposed two different solutions to gender inequality. The first solution was *socializing domestic work*, which means transferring work within the home to outside the home in an effort to bring value to it. The goal of socializing domestic work was not necessarily to have women stop doing domestic work, but to have domestic work valued the same as other work that took place in the public sphere and to share the burden that women alone have traditionally borne. The second solution was to provide monetary compensation for work performed within the home. Those who advocated this solution argued that women should not need to enter the paid workforce because they were already performing important work within the home. They contended that compensating women for their work within the home would bring attention to the value of domestic work, and, over time, it would come to be valued like other forms of work.

A primary difference between liberal feminism and Marxist feminism was in their perspectives of capitalism and gender inequality. Liberal feminists strived to be equal with men in the capitalist structure by obtaining equal access to high status and high paying jobs and equal opportunities to create individual wealth and power. For liberal feminists, capitalism was a system of voluntary exchange relations that women should be able to contribute to and benefit from equally with men. Marxist feminists argued gender inequality was built into the capitalist system. For women to be equal with men, the capitalist structure had to be changed. The first change would be to compensate women for their contributions to the capitalist system through their work in the home. Some Marxist feminists proposed additional social policies designed to support women's efforts to earn a living, such as state-funded childcare, extended maternity and paternity leave, and healthcare.

The Second Shift

Sociologist Arlie Hochschild studied the division of household labor among spouses with children in homes where both parents worked full time in the paid labor sphere. In most of the families Hochschild studied, women worked an eight hour day outside the home and then came home to work another shift of preparing dinner, cleaning the house, managing the family's social networks and schedules, and taking care of children. According to Hochschild, this evening and weekend work constituted women's *second shift*. Hochschild reported that only twenty percent of men in her study shared the second shift equally. In addition, men generally did more of the childrearing in terms of play and interaction whereas women did "the dirty work" of maintaining the children and the home. Hochschild noted that women were constantly trying to get everything done as quickly as possible in order to balance work and family. She argued this arrangement made women "villains" in their families by constantly hurrying the children and also made women victims of exhausted energy, sleep deprivation, high stress levels, and ongoing emotional torment associated with trying to balance work and family. In her later work *The Time Bind*, Hochschild argued women often work a *third shift*, in which they engage in emotional labor of trying to repair the damage to children created by their families' hectic schedules.

According to Hochschild, the evening and weekend work women performed in the home after an eight hour workday constituted a second shift. *(Shutterstock)*

Radical Feminism

Radical feminism began during second wave of feminist activism by scholars such as Marilyn French, Catharine MacKinnon, Andrea Dworkin, Adrienne Rich, and Mary Daly. Radical feminists argued that women's oppression in patriarchal societies is perpetuated through violence against women. Violence against women is rooted in patriarchal culture, which encourages and legitimizes male violence as a method of dominating and controlling women.

Although much violence against women is visible (rape, battery, and femicide), radical feminists believed "hidden" violence also contributed to women's subordination. Hidden violence includes excessive control over women's bodies through beauty standards, reproductive restrictions, and overemphasis on heterosexuality, much of which was (and continues to be) perpetuated through media. Radical feminists critiqued pornography to illustrate hidden violence. In pornography, women are often depicted as objects for men's pleasure and male violence against women is common. Such images perpetuated the idea that women are lesser than men and that male violence against women is a normal part of sexuality.

Radical feminists believed ending violence against women was necessary for the elimination of women's oppression. In their view, eliminating men's violence against women required transforming patriarchal culture from one that values "masculine" characteristics such as aggression, competition, and violence to one that reflects "feminine" characteristics, such as nurturance, peace, and intimacy. Radical feminists argued these characteristics are uniquely feminine not because women are biologically different than men, but because women do the majority of nurturing and childrearing. They further argued that men could assume these traits as well if they engaged in more nurturing activities. Radical feminists believed changing the value system was the most effective way to eliminate not only violence against women, but also other social problems such as poverty, war, and child abuse. This revolution had to occur not through war or violence but through peaceful transformation of the value system and norms of society.

Another component of radical feminist theory is the view that women's ability to reproduce is an incredible source of power. Radical feminists argued that women's ability to continue the existence of human life is the ultimate form of power but that patriarchal societies had diminished this power by claiming control over women's reproductive processes and proclaiming them sources of degradation rather than power. Women's emancipation thus entailed reclaiming the power embedded in women's bodies in the capacity to reproduce. Such a change would require redefining childbearing as a privilege rather than a burden and might entail providing rewards for childbearing, such as extended paid maternity leave.

Radical feminism significantly impacted the field of sociology. Whereas liberal feminists argued for inclusion of women in sociology, radical feminists argued that it was not enough to "add women and stir." As radical feminists explained, even though women had gained inclusion in sociology, the structure itself was still based on men's lives, values, and ways of thinking. Radical feminists asserted that when women conducted research through methods created by men, women continued to uphold structures of patriarchy because the methods of collecting data were based on male ways of understanding the world. Consequently, radical feminists sought to redefine the way research is practiced.

One change radical feminists advocated was the rejection of objectivity and implementation of reflexivity in research. **Objectivity** is a state of neutrality, or lack of personal judgment by the researcher. Radical feminists argued objectivity is impossible when studying social phenomena because sociological researchers live in the world they study. Rather than try or pretend to be objective, they argued, researchers should be reflexive. **Reflexivity** is a process of reflecting upon and acknowledging the personal impact researchers have on their research. Some things to consider are the researcher's social position based on gender, race, class, and sexuality, and personal experiences related to the research topic. Sandra Harding defined the reflexive approach as *strong objectivity* because it includes an in-depth reflection of the researcher's background and experiences on the research results rather than claiming false neutrality.

Intersectional Feminism

Intersectional feminism is a third wave feminist theory that emerged in the late 1980s, primarily as a critique of first and second wave theories. It is a theory developed by women of color, including Patricia Hill Collins, Barbara Smith, bell hooks, and Audre Lorde. Third wave feminists argued that although feminism brings awareness to gender inequality, it affords little attention to other forms of oppression such as racism, classism, and colonialism. Intersectional and indigenous feminists argued that women of color have different experiences from those of white women, a difference stemming from the intersections of gender, race, and class. They argued that first and second wave theories were not equipped to understand or eradicate minority women's oppression.

A key component of intersectional and other third wave feminist theories is *intersectional analysis*, which seeks to understand the ways in which gender, race, class, and sexuality interact to provide a unique set of social privileges, disadvantages, and experiences for diverse populations. Patricia Hill Collins conceptualized inequality in terms of a **matrix of domination**—a system of overlapping, intersecting inequalities based on individuals' configurations of race, class, and gender. Conceptualized in terms of a matrix, social privilege is not something an individual has or does not have but is something individuals have differential access to depending on their specific locations in the matrix. Collins argued that power has been traditionally thought of in terms of an **either/or dichotomy**, a system in which all cases naturally fit into one of two categories. Previous theories, for example, conceptualized power and privilege in dichotomous terms, as things individuals either have or do not have. Within this thought system, dominant group members are perceived as perpetuating the system to meet their interests whereas subordinate group members are perceived as opposing the system but succumbing to it due to their subordination. The matrix of domination conceptualizes power within a **both/and perspective** in which groups and individuals can belong to two or more categories at the same time. In the matrix of domination, a single individual need not be categorized as either oppressor or oppressed but can be perceived as both. For example, an individual might be privileged by virtue of race and social class but disadvantaged by virtue of gender and sexual orientation. By enjoying the privileges granted by race and social class, the individual contributes to the maintenance of the matrix of domination.

Intersectional feminists avoid placing one "ism," such as racism, sexism, or classism, above others. Instead, they conceptualize them in an interlocking matrix. They argue that people experience these intersecting inequalities differently, depending on their combination, and that this produces different social locations for different individuals. For example, black women in the United States may experience sexism and racism, but a wealthy black woman will have a different experience of class privilege and race and gender oppression than a poor black woman or middle-class Latina. With this in mind, intersectional feminists argue that feminist theories that do not include an analysis of race and class are inadequate for understanding the lives of the majority of the world's women.

The broader communities in which individuals live are also important to intersectional feminists. For example, whereas white women have benefited from the power and privilege of their white male fathers, brothers, husbands, and sons, the matrix of domination has prevented black women from benefitting from their association with an equivalently privileged group. Intersectional feminism also examine the ways in which inequality and oppression impact men of color. An intersectional analysis reveals that not only is sexism enacted differently based on race but racism is enacted differently based on sex. Black men, for example, are affected by a different set of stereotypes, disadvantages, and privileges than those which affect black women. Intersectional feminism also challenge the idea implicit in previous feminist theories that *all* men have greater power and privilege than *all* women. Intersectional feminists suggest men of color have not had the same structural resources or institutional power to oppress women as white men have had.

Intersectional feminists contend that some of the manifestations of oppression defined by previous feminist theories did not apply to some women of color. An example is reproduction. Liberal feminists argue that reproduction is an oppressive state for women because it interferes with women's abilities to compete with men in the workforce. Conversely, some intersectional feminists counter that black women historically have experienced the home and reproduction as spheres of power. During the era of African slavery in the United States, the home where black families gathered was the only space that was not directly ruled by a white master. Thus, the home was viewed as a liberating rather than oppressive space for many black women. For intersectional feminists, individuals are situated in the matrix of domination where their power or subjugation may shift depending on place, time, and context.

Womanism

Another third wave feminist theory is womanism, advanced by theorists such as Layli Phillips, Alice Walker, Clenora Hudson-Weems, and Chickwenye Okonjo-Ogunyemi. Womanism includes many concepts of intersectional feminism but deliberately avoids using the term feminism. As explained by Phillips, womanism is rooted in the black liberation movements from the Civil Rights era and other Africana liberation movements. For womanists, men are always included in the struggle to end oppression. Womanists argue that to isolate men (particularly men of color) from women's lives and struggles is not only near impossible but simply ineffective. The goal of womanism is to have entire communities join together to protest and overcome social injustices. Womanism differs from mainstream civil rights movements in that the struggle against sexism exists in tandem with race and class inequality.

Another component of womanism is the inclusion of spirituality. Womanist scholars assert that theory and research must include a spiritual component. They argue the spiritual realm is directly connected to human life and that the material and spiritual worlds are deeply intertwined. Thus, spiritualism is an important part of the research process for womanist scholars that must be integrated into scholarship.

Indigenous Feminism

Indigenous feminism, advanced by theorists such as Andrea Smith, Gloria Anzuldua, Trinh T. Minh-ha, Cherrie Moraga, and Haunani-Kay Trask, is similar to intersectional feminism and womanism in many ways, but applies specifically to indigenous populations. **Indigenous** applies to people who lived in the American and African continents before European colonization. Indigenous feminists contend that the word "feminism" may be a Western creation, but feminist theory and practice are deeply rooted in many indigenous cultures. Before European colonization, many indigenous communities lived cooperatively rather than under domination by one gender, race, or class. However, the feminist practices of indigenous women were historically ignored and often manipulated in Western writing to represent indigenous cultures in negative ways.

Part of the reverence for women evident in indigenous cultures stems from the association of women with nature and the earth. As explained by Haunani-Kay Trask, understanding the language of indigenous cultures is important in understanding the roles of women. For instance, in many indigenous languages there are no words for "ownership" or "owning the land." Instead, land is inherent to the people; people cannot exist without the land, and the land cannot exist without the people. And because women are viewed as connected to the land, they cannot be owned or dominated by others.

Indigenous feminism also critically examines the history of colonization. Smith's work posits that European colonizers enforced patriarchy to control Indigenous communities. Because most indigenous societies were not hierarchal in structure, colonizers had to first create hierarchies by instituting patriarchy. Thus, indigenous feminists believe patriarchy was uncommon in most

Indigenous Feminism

Feminism is a broad concept that comprises many different subgroups and theories. One growing area is known as indigenous feminism, or Native feminism. Indigenous feminists analyze the treatment of women in Native societies as they existed in the past compared to the treatment of women of Native descent in contemporary society. These feminists also study the role that violence against women played in the Western conquest of Native tribes and how Western ideas about women and sexuality have influenced the norms on reservations today. Some Native Americans criticize indigenous feminists, arguing that Native feminism is unnecessary because women traditionally enjoyed equality, positions of power, and respect in many Native societies. These critics accuse indigenous feminists of embracing white ideas and ignoring their own heritage, arguing that Native communities cannot focus on sexism because they are focusing on the more important and far-reaching issues of anticolonization and independence from Western values. Indigenous feminists counter that, regardless of how women were treated hundreds of years ago, the influence of Western patriarchy has resulted in the oppression of women of Native descent today. They further argue that ignoring the increased sexism and high rates of domestic violence against women on Native reservations hypocritically encourages colonialism and Western values by ignoring the egalitarian tradition of Native societies. Furthermore, indigenous feminists contend that it will be impossible for Native people to gain independence from Western values without first recognizing and eradicating the sexism that exists within their own communities. Rejecting the idea that they are ignoring their heritage or embracing Western values, indigenous feminists often refer to themselves as "feminists without apology."

Indigenous Nations, and that European colonizers introduced it into Native cultures. They further argue that rape was a tool used by colonizers to destroy indigenous communities. As colonizers raped indigenous women and took indigenous land, indigenous cultures and communities were destroyed.

SUMMARY

As with sociological theory in general, the development of feminist theories has taken place within sociohistorical context, impacted by the ideas and social circumstances of the time in which they are created. Early feminist theories explained gender inequality as a social phenomenon, arguing that women were biologically equal with men and therefore should be allowed to participate in education, paid labor, and politics. Women's entry into these institutions brought unforeseen challenges. Because the institutions were created for men and reflected male understandings of the world, the gender shift required new theories. As minority women gained a voice through inclusion in academia, feminist theories that incorporated studies of race and class, as well as gender, evolved.

Further Reading

Anzuldua, Gloria. *Borderlands/La Frontera: The New Mestiza*. San Francisco: Spinsters/
   AuntLute, 1999.
Collins, Patricia Hill, and Margaret Anderson. *Race, Class, & Gende,* 6th ed. Calif. : Thom-
   son Wadsworth, 2007
Friedan, Betty. *The Feminine Mystique*. New York: Dell, 1963.
Lorber, Judith. *Gender Inequality: Feminist Theories and Politics*, 2nd ed. Los Angeles: Rox-
   bury Publishing Company, 2001.
Phillips, Layli. *The Womanist Reader*. New York: Routledge, 2006.

CHAPTER 9

THEORIES OF EMANCIPATION

This chapter continues the discussion of theories of emancipation, which seek to provide equality for all. Here we summarize theories of race and ethnicity, postcolonialism, queer theory, and nonhuman theories.

THEORIES OF RACE AND ETHNICITY
Sociological theories of race and ethnicity seek to understand and explain the continuation of prejudice and racism in contemporary society. Whereas many social science theories consider prejudice originating from certain personality traits or other characteristics that reside within the prejudiced individual, sociological theories view race prejudice as a broader societal issue.

Group Positioning Theory
Group positioning theory was created by Herbert Blumer, the founder of symbolic interactionism. Blumer responded to previous social science theories that characterized prejudice as an individual's feeling of distaste directed at members of a minority group. Blumer argued such understandings were overly simplistic and failed to account for the social nature of prejudice. He argued that in order for prejudice to occur, individuals must have a *sense of group position*, in which they define themselves as members of a group and define certain others as members of a different group. Racial prejudice results from a set of ideas about where one's own group should stand in relation to other groups.

Blumer described four characteristics of dominant groups that contribute to racial prejudice. First is a feeling that the dominant group is superior to other groups. Second is a belief that members of other groups are intrinsically different from members of the dominant group. Third is the belief that members of the dominant group are entitled to certain rights, resources, and statuses to which other groups are not entitled. Fourth is a perception of threat that members of minority groups are attempting to take desired resources from the dominant group. Taken together, prejudice results from a dominant group's perceptions of itself as a distinct group with interests that require protection from other groups.

Contemporary race scholar Lawrence Bobo extended Blumer's group positioning theory. Bobo developed the concept of **laissez-faire racism**, the belief that racial inequality results from a lack of work ethic among blacks. Bobo argued that the content of prejudicial thinking is related to the social conditions in which dominant groups' believe they need to protect their interests. Bobo proposed that **old-fashioned racism**—the belief that whites are biologically superior to blacks—developed under certain conditions that helped whites protect their interests. In particular, the idea that blacks are biologically inferior to whites justified the exploitation of slaves for use in agricultural work in the southeastern United States. Once slavery was abolished it was no longer necessary for whites to define blacks as biologically inferior. In the free market, racial inequality could be explained as resulting from racial differences in work ethic. Thus, Bobo observed, dominant white ideas were transformed from *old-fashioned racism*, belief in biological superiority of whites, to *laissez-faire racism*, belief that racial inequality results from a lack of work ethic among blacks. According to Bobo, this shift does not reflect a change simply in whites' attitudes but a change in whites' group interests. Laissez-faire racism supports whites' group interests by explaining blacks' failure to achieve racial equality in the free market system in a way that blames blacks rather than whites or the system. These beliefs correspond with reluctance among whites to support programs and policies designed to alleviate racial inequality, which helps whites protect their interests.

In Bobo's view, the components of prejudice Blumer outlined to describe dominant groups' attitudes toward minorities could also be applied to minority groups' feelings toward dominant groups and to prejudice among minority groups. He found in his research that prejudice is not simply held by the dominant group against subordinate groups but that subordinate groups also hold prejudices against each other.

Symbolic Racism

The theory of symbolic racism was developed by Donald Kinder and David Sears. Symbolic racism is based on the observation that *old-fashioned racism*

—overt negative feelings and attitudes toward African Americans based on perceived biological inferiority—is declining. **Symbolic racism** posits that although old-fashioned racism is declining, there is still an underlying animosity among whites toward blacks. Many whites hold negative stereotypes of blacks and perceive blacks as violating longstanding American values such as hard work, independence, and individual responsibility. These stereotypes are held in conjunction with the idea that blacks no longer experience discrimination in U.S. society. Consequently, the perceived solution to racial inequality is for blacks to work harder and not depend on government intervention. Thus, symbolic racism is a combination of negative feelings toward blacks and the belief that blacks violate core American values, which together result in continuing racial inequality. Like laissez-faire racism, the consequence of symbolic racism is that many whites are unwilling to support government policies that work to reduce racial inequalities.

Color-blind Racism
The theory of color-blind racism was developed by Leslie G. Carr and elaborated upon by Eduardo Bonilla-Silva, among others. The concept of *color blindness* refers to the operation of programs, policies, and social actions without consideration of race. Color blindness was originally advocated within the Civil Rights movement by leaders such as Martin Luther King, Jr., who argued that African Americans should not be denied certain rights and privileges because of their race. Thus, King and other Civil Rights leaders advocated color blindness to alleviate racial discrimination.

Contemporary race scholars such as Carr and Bonilla-Silva suggested that color-blind ideologies in the post-Civil Rights era perpetuate racial inequality, resulting in a new form of racism termed color-blind racism. **Color-blind racism** is a cultural ideology based on the belief that race is no longer significant in U.S. society and therefore opposes social policies and programs designed to alleviate racial inequality. The argument among those who espouse a color-blind ideology is that programs that take race into account, such as Affirmative Action, perpetuate racism by making race matter. Because the underlying belief in this group is that race is no longer significant in society, they perceive such policies are not only unnecessary but problematic.

Most race scholars, however, argue that color-blind ideology constitutes a new form of racism because it perpetuates racial inequality. All social indicators show race is still significant in U.S. society, determining everything from individuals' probability of being stopped by police to the kind of education they receive and type of career they will have to the kind of medical treatment they receive and their chances of living a long and healthy life. Although there has been a decline in overt racist acts, racial minorities continue to be systematically disadvantaged through all major social institutions. Therefore, an

Symbolic and Color-blind Racism

While some overt forms of racism, such as Jim Crow laws, no longer exist in the United States, racism is far from extinct in contemporary society. One of the most strongly held American ideals is the belief that equal opportunities are available to all members of society. In order to rationalize inequalities, therefore, individuals may attribute negative qualities to a minority group. For example, rather than accept that equal opportunity may be a myth, certain individuals may assert that African Americans earn lower average income than whites because they are lazy or less ambitious. This subtle and sometimes unconscious racism is known as symbolic racism. While not actively denying a minority equal opportunity, symbolic racism can convince individuals that inequality is explainable and justified, and can therefore prevent equality from becoming a reality. Furthermore, symbolic racism allows people in positions of power to underestimate and ignore oppression. This is similar to color-blind racism, another subtle form of racism. Color-blind racism occurs when individuals claim that race is not important to them, so they do not notice race—in other words, they are "color blind." By refusing to acknowledge race at all, color-blind racism ignores racial inequalities, much like symbolic racism. People who practice color-blind or symbolic racism are often unaware that they are exhibiting racism and may in fact believe that their beliefs are beneficial to minorities. Being aware of inequalities in America and accepting that race does play an important role in socioeconomic trends can help combat these subtle but harmful types of racism.

ideology that ignores these inequalities and declines support for policies designed to alleviate them contributes to their continuation.

Critical Race Theory

Critical race theory (CRT) was created in the 1970s by Derrick Bell, a scholar in the field of critical legal studies. CRT was developed as an approach to analyze racial biases in law. As a social theory, CRT builds on the work of critical theorists to understand and attempt to alleviate race inequality. Like critical theory, CRT focuses on the roles of knowledge and ideology as they pertain to the creation and perpetuation of racial inequality. Also like critical theory, CRT is based on the notion of *praxis*, theory for the purpose of social action. Although CRT was originally created to analyze white/black inequalities, it has led to the creation of other variations that examine racism toward and within other groups. Among these new theories are Latina/o Critical Theory (LatCrit), Asian Critical Theory (AsianCrit), and Critical Whiteness Studies (WhiteCrit).

CRT argues racism is a normal part of U.S. society. That is, racism is a built-in feature of the social system that operates in such a way that it appears ordinary and goes unnoticed by most people, particularly whites. Thus, racism is part of the ordinary operations of society rather than an exceptional or infrequent event.

One way racism is built into the fabric of U.S. society is through dominant ideas about what counts as knowledge. CRT argues that current methods of validating knowledge devalue the knowledge and experiences of racial minorities. For example, historical analyses traditionally focus on official documents to provide information about "historical facts." Whatever is written in official documents is considered true. However, this method of recordkeeping was created by whites, who have historically had more power to document "facts" than other groups. Black slaves were often forbidden to learn to read and write and therefore shared their experiences through oral storytelling. Because the written word is considered "knowledge" and oral storytelling is not, what we know about slavery disproportionately reflects what white people chose to write about it.

Critical race theorists contend that much of what passes as knowledge in U.S. society is comprised of **majoritorian stories**, truth claims generated by those with race privilege. Rather than representing a neutral or objective "truth," majoritorian stories reflect assumptions, perspectives, and world-views of those privileged by race. Underlying this argument is the notion of **white privilege**, recognition of advantages granted to all whites, knowingly or unknowingly, that derives from the system of racism in U.S. society. Critical race theorists argue majoritorian stories are often told from the perspective of "race neutrality," suggesting race does not play a role in the viewpoint of the storyteller. However, it is only whites who can claim to be "racially neutral," and the claim of race neutrality is part of white privilege. CRT points out that everyone has a race, and therefore there is no "race neutral" perspective. However, the group with the most power—those who maintain white privilege—is granted the privilege of naming their perspective "neutral." Thus, an African American perspective is considered a racial perspective whereas a white perspective is considered a neutral perspective. This kind of logic, critical race theorists argue, is embedded in majoritorian stories and perpetuates white privilege and racial inequality. Moreover, critical race theorists argue, social science often engages in the telling of majoritorian stories through theories that blame minorities for racial inequalities and research methods that overlook minorities' knowledge and experiences.

CRT uses alternative methods for creating knowledge and conveying information. One method is *storytelling*, creating fictional or nonfictional stories to make visible the ways racism operates in U.S. society. The goal of storytelling in CRT is to document and validate the distinctive knowledge and experiences of racial minorities and challenge dominant ideologies. Some CRT theorists refer to this as *counter-storytelling* to emphasize that these stories stand in contrast to majoritorian stories, although counter-stories do not need to be written in direct opposition to majoritorian stories. Instead, they can be used to explore new themes, experiences, or knowledge that are excluded from majoritorian stories. CRT storytelling can comprise serious stories of oppression and resistance or use humor and political satire. The use of storytelling in CRT is prompted by the idea that social reality is constructed by individuals in society. Through storytelling, CRT theorists create and promote new social realities.

POSTCOLONIALISM

Postcolonialism is a body of social theory that is critical of the colonizing activities of Western societies. **Colonialism** refers to political domination of one nation by another, which benefits the dominant nation at the subordinate nation's expense. Colonialism typically refers to the expansion of Western European control over nations in Africa, Asia, and the Americas, particularly from the late 15th to the 20th centuries. **Imperialism** refers to the set of ideas and beliefs that support colonialism, or the policy involved in a nation maintaining colonial control over another. **Postcolonialism** is an interdisciplinary body of social theory that is critical of colonial rule, particularly the impact of colonialism on native cultures.

Edward Said

Edward Said is one of the founders of postcolonial thought. In his book *Orientalism*, Said analyzed Western European history and literary texts to extract Western views of Eastern societies, or the "Orient." Said argued the Orient exists only in Western imagination because the West lumps together diverse societies from all of Asia and the Middle East and does not distinguish between them. In addition, Said contended that Western cultures characterize the Orient as backward, barbaric, and uncivilized. He also objected to the West's interpretation of Eastern spiritual beliefs and practices, which were characterized as dominated by belief in false entities and mysticism, the products of uncritical and irrational beings. Through such portrayals, Said argued, the Orient and its people have been characterized as "Other." This view of the Oriental Other is juxtaposed (presented as opposite to) the view of the "Occident," which represents the Western Self and portrays Westerners as progressive, advanced, and civilized, with ideas and actions that are critical and rational. Said argued that these disparate portrayals allow people in Western societies to dominate those in Eastern societies. In addition, those in Western societies have had the power to define and describe Eastern Others who have not had the power to define themselves.

Subaltern Studies

Subaltern studies is a body of postcolonial theory that is critical of the works of Said and other postcolonial theorists for focusing solely on the viewpoint of the oppressor. Subaltern theorists argue such theories privilege those in Western societies by theorizing oppression from the dominant perspective, which they argue contributes to the marginalization of those who are oppressed by colonialism because it denies them a voice. These theorists advocate theory and research from the perspective of the oppressed. Subaltern studies focus on the responses and resistance of groups who are oppressed by colonial rule. Gayatri Spivak furthered this perspective, arguing that a study of resistance must include those societies or groups that do not have the power to vocalize their opposition and thereby resist oppression in silence.

QUEER THEORY

Queer theory is a branch of emancipatory theory that explores social and political definitions of gender and sexuality. Queer theorists analyze the ways in which certain expressions of gender and sexuality are framed as normal and others deviant. The term "queer" does not refer to any specific type of person or behavior, but instead refers to whatever society considers the opposite of normal. Just as there can be no teacher without a student, or no old without young, a thing can only be queer when there is an established norm.

Queer theory begins with the observation that contemporary U.S. society is **heteronormative**, meaning the dominant ideology holds that all people fall into the distinct categories of either male or female and that heterosexuality is normal. In a heteronormative society, anything that does not fit within heteronormativity is considered queer, including homosexuality, bisexuality, transgendered individuals, asexuality, and people who are born without distinct male or female features. In a heteronormative society, people typically assume the categories male, female, and heterosexuality are normal and natural—that there is no other "natural" way to conceive of gender and sexuality. However, queer theorists point out that heteronormativity is not universal. Different societies have different ideas about how many gender categories there are, what forms of sexuality are "normal," and what is queer. Therefore, queer theorists argue, gender and sexuality are products of society and culture rather than nature.

Foundational Theories

Although queer theory officially emerged during the 1990s, groundwork was laid decades earlier by Michel Foucault who wrote extensively about normative and deviant sexuality. Foucault theorized that the concept of sexual orientation is a product of *discourse*, official language. Like mental illness, homosexuality did not exist as a concept until psychiatric discourse created it. Hundreds of years ago, no term existed for homosexual males. Instead, sex between men was descriptively referred to as sodomy and was merely considered different from other types of sex. Individuals who engaged in sodomy were not viewed any differently from individuals who did not. As Judeo-Christian traditions began to dominate Western societies, heteronormative views began to take hold. As heterosexuality became defined as the norm, homosexuality became defined as abnormal, and sodomy widely became considered sinful. Later, with the advancement of scientific medicine, especially psychiatry, early psychiatrists defined homosexuality as a psychiatric disorder. The definition of sodomy as sinful was replaced with the definition of sodomy as abnormal and deviant. Foucault pointed out that this switch from sinful to deviant was a change only in the way homosexuality was framed; the message that homosexuality is against the norm remained the same.

Foucault also asserted that the psychiatric view of homosexuality as a psychiatric disorder led to the conception of a *homosexual subject*, an individual who is fundamentally different from people who are heterosexual. As noted above, before the discursive creation of the "homosexual," men who had sex with other men were simply viewed as regular people who engaged in acts of sodomy. Although these acts themselves were later defined as sinful, the people who engaged in them were not defined as fundamentally different from those who did not. After the discursive creation of the "homosexual," Foucault argued, it became possible to perceive individuals who engaged in sodomy as intrinsically different from those who did not. That is, the entire personhood of these individuals came to be defined by their sexuality. Later queer theorists expanded this idea, pointing out that similar definitions of personhood are not attributed to individuals based on other sexual practices. For example, a gay male in a monogamous relationship may engage in sexual practices that are most similar to those of a straight male in a monogamous relationship when compared to gay and straight males that engage in promiscuous sexuality. However, psychiatric discourse defined gay and straight as socially significant categories and did not define monogamous and promiscuous as equally significant. Therefore, monogamous and promiscuous gay males are perceived as members of the same category or group (gay) and monogamous and promiscuous straight males are perceived as members of another category or group (straight) even though their respective sexual practices (monogamy or promiscuity) make them more similar to the monogamous or promiscuous members of the other category or group.

According to Foucault, this is how discourse works. Because the concept of being gay did not exist prior to this *discursive formation*, there were no homosexual or heterosexual people before they were created through discourse. Thus, Foucault argued, sexual orientation is strictly a social construction. Many queer theorists support this idea that being gay is not an objective quality but an identity created by society. Without the social construction of sexual orientation, people would not consider their choice of sexual partners as a part of their personal identity. This idea is known as the **constructivist** view. Another way to understand the constructivist view of sexuality is to consider that a person cannot be a member of a club or organization that does not exist. No matter how strongly a person may have supported the Bill of Rights, that person could not be a member of the American Civil Liberties Union (ACLU) prior to its official formation. Though the individual's actions and beliefs would be the same before and after the creation of the ACLU, it was not until after the formation that this person could gain an identity as an ACLU member. Likewise, prior to the discursive formation of sexual orientation, a person may have engaged in sexual relations with a member of the same sex, but sexual orientation was not an available identity.

Other queer theorists view sexual orientation as a natural attribute that it is an integral part of an individual's identity, a theoretical construct that is referred to as **essentialism**. Essential qualities are those without which a person would no longer be the same person. For example, if you remove the tail of a cat, it is still a cat, so a tail is an inessential quality. It can be difficult to ascertain precisely what qualities are essential to any object or individual, and there may be no objective answer, which is why there is a debate among queer theorists on this subject. However, essentialists believe that if a person's sexual orientation were removed, his or her identity and personality would be altered. Constructivists counter that a person's actions or behavior are just as likely to remain the same even without the label of a sexual orientation.

Contemporary Queer Theory

Queer theory is not limited to discussions of sexuality but is also used to analyze gender roles in society. Heteronormative societies hold that all people are either male or female, with expected guidelines of behavior for each gender. However, not all people are born clearly male or female. Approximately 1.7 percent of individuals in the United States are born *intersex*, with various combinations of female and male anatomical features. In contemporary U.S. society, parents of intersexed children are often encouraged to "choose" a gender for their children, who will then undergo surgery to remove or rebuild the anatomical parts that do not conform to those of the chosen gender. This can be difficult for individuals who are assigned one gender but ultimately feel they should be the other. In a similar vein, some individuals who are born with clearly male or female anatomy feel they were born into the wrong body. These *transgendered* individuals struggle with the female or male gender they were given at birth and may long to have that gender reversed.

Even among individuals who are satisfied with their gender, societal pressure to conform to certain behavioral norms is very powerful. From birth, girls and boys are trained to like certain toys and colors and are expected to act in certain ways; they are also to taught to recognize that there are social consequences for breaking the rules. Queer theory questions the rigidity of gender in contemporary society, asking why individuals with an undefined gender must be defined, rather than accepted, and why it is considered unacceptable for girls to act like boys and vice versa. Judith Butler argued that gender is not an objective reality but a collective, sustained narrative of many people behaving a certain way over time. Butler pointed out that boys and girls engage in

MSM and WSW

Many men and women reject labels of gay or homosexual in an effort to forgo an identity based on their sexual preferences. Instead, they refer to themselves descriptively as "men who have sex with men" (MSM) and "women who have sex with women" (WSW). This choice exemplifies the essentialist and constructivist viewpoints. MSM and WSW are constructivists, refusing to accept a label constructed by society. It is important to note that refusing to accept a socially constructed identity is not a denial of one's behaviors or feelings. MSM and WSW may engage in behaviors that are ultimately no different from those of people who identify themselves as gay or lesbian. It is the label itself that is rejected, not the behavior signified by the label. Furthermore, the terms gay and homosexual both signify a rigid sexuality, one that is just as rigid as heterosexuality. By rejecting these labels, MSM and WSW avoid limiting themselves to predefined rules about whom they can and cannot be attracted to.

Same-sex couple hold hands at a marriage march. *(Wikipedia)*

repetitive actions that mimic acceptable behavior for their gender, thus learning how to *act* in a way that is considered correct in their society. These gender performances continually perpetuate what is considered normal, casting other behaviors as abnormal or deviant.

Michael Warner also questioned the validity of normalcy in his book *The Trouble with Normal*. Warner argued that "normal" is an arbitrary statistical distinction and that there is no real reason to consider anything normal. He suggested it may be harmful for people outside the norm to try to conform and advocated instead for expanding the definition of what is considered normal. Steven Seidman warned that trying to understand people outside the norm may in fact devalue them. He explained that the first step of studying a person who is outside the norm is labeling that person as outside the norm, which poses the danger of making that individual feel inferior rather than just different.

Though a relatively new branch of sociological theory, queer theory is a rapidly expanding niche, particularly in contemporary U.S. society. Advancements in technology are making it easier for transgendered individuals to undergo treatments that make it possible for them to live their lives in the bodies in which they feel comfortable, and debates regarding same-sex marriage and having gays serve in the military without having to conceal their sexual identity are regularly in the news.

NONHUMAN THEORIES

Though sociology most commonly deals with humans, some sociologists study human interactions with nonhuman entities. Two examples of such studies involve nonhuman animals and the natural environment, both of which are a part of daily life in human society.

Theories of Nonhuman Animals

Nonhuman animals are a fundamental part of society. Animals serve tangible functions, such as providing humans with food or clothing, or assisting human labor. Some provide entertainment or companionship as pets; others serve as research subjects. Animals also serve intangible functions, such as symbols that represent specific emotions or personality traits. For example, lions represent courage and owls represent wisdom. Even our language reflects the influence of animals on human society; "six-dog night," "hold your horses," and "eat like a pig" are just a few common phrases in which animals are used to convey certain meanings.

One theoretical approach to human-animal interactions uses Marx's analysis of the exploitation of factory workers. Marx argued that exploitation in factories is an integral part of capitalism. In order to increase profits, factory owners must cut costs and strive to get the most out of their workers. Animals have long been used to help humans work and as natural resources for products such as food and clothing. In many ways, animals are means of production in and of themselves. Since animals are not paid for their work, people who rely on animals for their livelihoods must find other ways to decrease costs and increase profits. Costs can be decreased by reducing the quality of living conditions for animals, using lower-quality feed, or increasing the number of animals in a given space to maximize capacity. Such practices allow capitalists to reduce costs and increase profits, but they also increase the exploitation of animals. In this way, a Marxist lens is used to understand the exploitation of animals for capitalist profits.

Another way of analyzing human-animal interactions draws from feminist theories. The oppression of women in a patriarchal society can be related to the oppression of animals by humans. For example, men and women are often associated with different animals, which are used to symbolize gender differences. Men are often referred to as wolves or snakes, which emphasize a patriarchal view of men as predatory, strong, and powerful. Women are sometimes referred to as kittens or bunnies, words which call to mind defenseless or weak qualities. At other times women may be referred to as foxes or minxes, words that suggest women are manipulative or untrustworthy.

Feminist theorist Carol J. Adams discussed the link between the treatment of animals and women in U.S. society in her book *The Sexual Politics of Meat*. Adams wrote about the use of female sexuality to sell animal products. She argued that women are consumed visually to promote the literal consumption of animals. A common example is the frequent coupling of scantily-clad waitresses in restaurants that feature chicken wings. Underscoring the idea that eating lots of meat is manly or masculine, Adams included many visual examples of advertisements for food that compare body parts of animals to those of women or make use of sexual innuendos and puns.

Environmental Theories

In contemporary Western societies, humans are often far removed from the natural environment. Many live in urban and suburban areas with little green space. Although every product humans consume comes from nature, this fact is often difficult to see once the product is packaged and put on a shelf in a store. Nevertheless, society relies on nature every day, and also heavily impacts it.

The Marxist approach is one theoretical lens that can be applied to human-environment interactions. A cornerstone of Marx's theories is the cyclic exchange of commodities (C) and money (M) in the M-C-M and C-M-C exchanges described earlier in this book. Environmental sociologist Allan Schnaiberg referred to these exchanges as the **treadmill of production** (M-C-M) and the **treadmill of consumption** (C-M-C).

Like the M-C-M and C-M-C exchanges, the treadmills of production and consumption cannot exist without each other. Without production, there would be no commodities to consume, and without consumers to purchase the increasing number of commodities available, production would stop. Furthermore, the treadmills increase in speed and size as they feed into each other. The result of this, environmentally, is faster and greater resources used to create commodities, and faster and greater production of waste that must be disposed of.

The problem with the treadmills of production and consumption is that natural resources are often finite. For example, increasing numbers of

For the Dogs

Few animals are more entrenched in the lives of humans than dogs. One of the earliest domesticated animals, dogs have shared a close relationship with humans for thousands of years. Early nomadic and hunter-gatherer humans enjoyed a mutually beneficial relationship with dogs, with humans receiving companionship and protection from dogs in exchange for food and affection. Some scientific studies suggest humans and dogs in fact co-evolved, and certainly, humans have played a significant role in the development of the hundreds of different dog breeds that exist today. Millions of Americans share their homes with dogs, but the nature of the relationship has evolved over time. Throughout history, dogs alternated between symbolizing aristocracy and servants. While humans and dogs continue to benefit from their partnership, there are interesting sociological implications related to owning a particular type of dog. For example, small dogs such as toy poodles and Chihuahuas are often viewed as feminine and may suggest a wealthy lifestyle. In contrast, bull terriers, commonly known as pit bulls, are often seen as masculine dogs, representing a rough, street-worn life. These symbolic meanings are projected onto dogs by humans, regardless of the sex or personality of an individual animal.

Marine Sergeant pets his dog. *(Wikipedia)*

landfills correspond with a decreasing amount of land to use for new landfills. As the treadmills of production and consumption increase in speed and size, they diminish the availability of the resources they need to survive. This scramble to keep the treadmills going even as they undermine themselves is known as the **growth machine**. A growth machine encourages any kind of economic development, constantly pushing for "bigger" and "more," with little or no regard for environmental consequences. In a growth machine, a conflict arises between two of Marx's other ideas, use value and exchange value. For example, to maximize its use value, a piece of land might be turned into a public park. To maximize its exchange value, the same piece of land might be used to build condominiums. The constant pressure of the growth machine and the treadmill of production frequently results in exchange value winning out and environmental interests losing.

Environmental sociology also draws upon Max Weber's work to theorize the relationship between religion and human interactions with the environment. Weber demonstrated that the Protestant ethic corresponded with ever-increasing production and fixation with material goods. This ethic has real implications for the natural environment. Prior to the spread of Christianity many societies practiced pagan religions that emphasized spiritual ties with nature. Nomadic and hunter-gatherer societies relied on nature directly for food and shelter in order to survive, so nature was thanked when it was used, and it was used efficiently. In contrast, Christianity teaches that humans are the dominant species on the Earth and thus dominate everything living on it. Furthermore, as technology progressed, the direct reliance of humans on nature decreased. Therefore, Christianity was coupled with the advancement of technology, and the idea that humans are dominant over nature became a standard Western norm. Environmental sociologist Riley Dunlap called this dominance viewpoint the **Human Exemptionalist Paradigm** (HEP). Individuals operating under the HEP see humans as separate from and superior to nature. They believe they are exempt from consequences that may arise from tampering with the natural environment. The result is a disregard for the environment and natural resources. The alternative to the HEP is the **New Ecological Paradigm** (NEP). This perspective views humans as existing within Earth's ecosystems rather than outside them. Dunlap suggested that if humanity is to stop its rapid surge toward environmental destruction, a shift from the dominant HEP to the more environmentally friendly NEP must take place.

Feminist theorists have taken this idea a step further, pointing out that while Christianity gives humans dominion over the Earth, it also gives men dominion over women. The theory that draws a parallel between these two points is called *eco-feminism*. Eco-feminists argue that the dominant society views men as "normal" and women as deviant, or "Other." Similarly, the pro-growth HEP of the United States views civilization and development as normal, while untamed nature is the deviant Other. Feminist sociologist Simone de Beauvoir cautioned that highlighting the link between the oppression of women and the environment only strengthens their sense of Otherness. In contrast, eco-feminists believe equality for women and a positive relationship with the environment go hand in hand.

SUMMARY

Theories of race and ethnicity, postcolonialism, queer theory, and nonhuman theories analyze power relationships between dominant groups and their subordinates. Although each body of theory has its own primary focus, the overall goal of all of the theories is to bring emancipation to all oppressed beings. In this way, emancipatory theories share theoretical ideas and insights and work toward common goals.

Further Reading

Armstrong, Susan J., and Richard G. Botzler. *The Animal Ethics Reader.* New York: Routledge, 2008.

Cuff, E. C., W. W. Sharrock, and D. W. Francis. *Perspectives in Sociology,* 5th ed. London: Routledge, 2006.

Delgado, Richard, and Jean Stefancic. *Critical Race Theory: An Introduction.* New York: New York University Press, 2001.

Dunlap, Riley E., Frederick H. Buttel, Peter Dickens, and August Gijswijt. *Sociological Theory and the Environment: Classical Foundations, Contemporary Insights.* Lanham, Md.: Rowman & Littlefield, 2002.

Sears, David O., Jim Sidanius, and Lawrence Bobo. *Racialized Politics: The Debate about Race in America.* Chicago: University of Chicago Press, 2000.

Warner, Michael. *Fear of a Queer Planet: Queer Politics and Social Theory.* Minneapolis, Minn.: University of Minnesota Press. 1993.

CHAPTER 10

THEORY AND
THE REAL WORLD

As sociological theories develop and change over time, they reflect broader changes in the social contexts and thought patterns in which they are created. Thus, social theory will continue to change and develop as societies change and develop. Social theories help us understand the characteristics, dynamics, and inner workings of societies. However, social theories do more than just help us understand the world around us; they guide research practices, inform political activism, and shape public policies.

THEORY AND RESEARCH

Sociological research is always impacted by theory. The ways researchers approach topics, the research questions they develop, the procedures they use to collect and analyze data, and how they interpret results are all shaped by theories. Social science research can generally be divided into the categories of *quantitative research,* which uses numbers to represent sociological phenomena and analyzes them using statistics, and *qualitative research*, which focuses on description and deep understanding. Quantitative researchers rely on scientific sensibilities to guide their research. They strive to maintain *objectivity*, a state of personal neutrality in the research, so as not to interfere with the research results. This form of research is based on the presumption that a real, objective world exists "out there" and can be studied. The idea that social researchers can study an objective world and draw true conclusions from their research is referred to as *positivism*.

Although quantitative research dominates the field of sociology, it is contested by many theories. For example, Blumer's theory of symbolic interactionism advocated qualitative methods. Blumer argued that society is made up of individuals acting and interacting based on their interpretations of things, and a study of society must focus on just that: people's interpretations of things. This focus calls for in-depth analysis of people's perceptions, definitions, symbols, and descriptions of the social world. Blumer's theory was based on the idea of **relativity**, that what is real varies depending on the knower. That is, what one person may perceive as true, another may perceive as false. According to symbolic interactionism, it is not important or possible to know which person holds the "correct" understanding of reality because each individual lives according to what she or he believes is correct. Therefore, an understanding of society results not from trying to understand some objective truth "out there" but an understanding of the subjective truths people live by in everyday life.

Phenomenologists provide a similar critique of scientific methods in sociology. Phenomenologists believe all human experience is mediated by human consciousness, and therefore, humans operate in a subjective life-world. This logic is counter to that used in science, which seeks to uncover facts about the concrete, objective world that is assumed to exist outside the individual. Furthermore, as human beings, scientists are not able to transcend their own life-world. Science, however, requires such a transcendence because the goal of science is to study the concrete world that exists independent of the life-world. If humans cannot escape the life-world, they cannot verify that an objective world exists and therefore cannot study it scientifically. Moreover, assuming that humans operate in a life-world rather than an external world and that the goal of sociology is to understand human life, then the focus of sociology should be the life-world.

Symbolic interactionist and phenomenological theories have led to the creation of a branch of qualitative sociology known as **naturalism**, which seeks to understand participants' interpretations of their lived experiences. Naturalists argue sociological research should be conducted in the locations where social life naturally takes place, such as people's homes, workplaces, and city streets rather than fabricated locations, such as laboratories. In naturalism, researchers need to "go there," to the places ordinary people conduct their lives. It is within these natural settings that researchers should observe the ordinary interactions among people to gain an understanding of the people's regular lives. Through such observation, researchers will learn the organization, hierarchies, symbols, meanings, and experiences that are important to the people they seek to understand. Naturalistic researchers may also conduct in-depth interviews to gain a deeper understanding of the personal experiences and interpretations of individuals. The result of naturalistic research is *ethnography*, an in-depth analysis of a small group of people's everyday lives.

Feminist Research Methods

Feminists and other emancipatory sociologists argue that scientific reasoning in sociology reflects dominant groups' ways of thinking and promotes subordination of others by misrepresenting their experiences. In response to this reasoning, feminists have created a set of research principles known as *feminist research methods* that largely contradict the principles of science. They begin by questioning scientific reasoning, which posits that researchers should study phenomena that do not impact them personally so they may maintain neutrality. Feminist researchers counter with the argument that personal experience is a source of knowledge and that researchers can provide better research insights into phenomena they have personally experienced. Secondly, feminist researchers argue against traditional interviewing methods in which researchers ask questions and participants provide answers as such methods create distance and hierarchy between researchers and participants. Feminists advocate equality in the researcher-participant relationship, particularly in data collection that involves personal topics. Equality can be created through mutual disclosure, empathy, and intimacy in the research interview. A third point that feminist researchers work to promote is an ethics of caring. They argue that researchers have a responsibility to promote the well-being of their participants rather than just gain information from them. To accommodate this view, feminist research incorporates sharing information and advice with participants. In a fourth point, feminists contend that researchers are accountable for the knowledge they create through their research efforts. If a researcher promotes knowledge that is harmful to a particular group, feminists argue, that researcher is responsible for the damage done as a result of the research conducted.

Ethnomethodologists also use qualitative methods but rely on a different set of assumptions than symbolic interactionists or phenomenologists. Ethnomethodologists view the social world as constantly being constructed and negotiated through ongoing interactions. Thus, how an individual interprets a "lived experience" will vary depending on the context in which the person is telling the story. In contrast to the naturalistic view that individuals have lived experiences that they interpret in certain ways, ethnomethodologists posit that individuals' interpretations of their lived experiences unfold as they go about their daily lives. Whereas an individual may interpret something a certain way, that same individual may interpret the same thing differently at a later time. Therefore, sociological researchers cannot capture individuals' lived experiences and must analyze instead their stories or *narratives* of experience. Rather than focus on *what* individuals interpret as their experiences, ethnomethodologists analyze *how* the narratives are assembled. This perspective is associated with **social constructionism**, which views the world as socially constructed through individuals' interactions and analyzes how people construct their social lives.

Emancipatory sociologists are also critical of scientific methodologies in sociology. Much quantitative research examines and compares the *mean*, or average of something. For example, an examination of church attendance might look at the average number of times individuals attend church in a year. Sociologists might compare the means for different groups to see if certain groups attend church more often than other groups. In order to make statistical comparisons, sociologists need a certain number of individuals representative of each group, something that is difficult to achieve. There may be enough individuals who are white, black, and Hispanic in the sample to compare these groups, but there are typically not enough who are Asian, Native American, or Middle Eastern to include these groups in the comparison. These groups would be excluded from the study because they are not large enough to make statistically significant comparisons.

Emancipatory sociologists argue this exclusion from research contributes to these groups' subordination in society. First, exclusion suggests these groups are not important in society. Second, knowledge created about a particular topic includes only perspectives and experiences of dominant groups. Consequently, little information is available about subordinate groups, and dominant groups' perspectives continue to be considered the norm. Emancipatory sociologists argue nonscientific methods are necessary for understanding the knowledge and experiences of oppressed groups.

THEORY AND ACTIVISM

Sociological theory is also used to inform **political activism**, organized actions that seek to create social change. Critical and emancipatory sociology are based on the notion of *praxis*, theory for the purpose of social change. The idea of praxis is that all knowledge is political, so theory and research that creates knowledge that aims to emancipate oppressed people is in itself political activism. Here the knowledge itself is used to create change by exposing the ways domination is perpetuating and working to change ideologies that support domination.

Sociological theories are also used in more traditional political activism, such as creating political organizations, recruiting members, and arranging protests. The relationship between theory and activism has always mattered to sociologists. Karl Marx, for example, advocated labor movements and the formation of labor unions. At the time Marx was writing, there were no labor laws, so people worked long hours for little pay. The formation of labor unions brought about significant social changes, including minimum wages, child labor laws, workplace safety regulations, overtime pay, and weekends as nonwork days. Other classical theorists also engaged in political activism. Emile Durkheim was active in promoting educational reform in France. W.E.B. Du Bois was active in promoting civil rights for African Americans and was one of the founders of the National Association for the Advancement of Colored People (NAACP). Women sociologists at the University of Chicago founded Hull House, an organization that provided social and educational opportunities to recent immigrants.

Social theory is also used to inform political activism today. Social organizations such as the NAACP, the National Organization for Women (NOW), and the National Gay and Lesbian Task Force put theory into action through their outreach activities. Whereas sociological theorists provide the knowledge and understanding of social forces that contribute to social inequalities, outreach organizations use this knowledge to promote social change. Sociological knowledge can be used to identify areas of society that need improvement and to gauge public perceptions to determine whether or not a particular political policy or program will garner support or opposition. For example, recent research has demonstrated that high school students who are perceived to be gay or lesbian are disproportionately targets of bullying. Antibullying legislation has been enacted and used in conjunction with programs that promote tolerance and understanding for sexual diversity.

A newer branch of sociology is **public sociology**, in which sociological work is created for a general audience. Public sociology is contrasted with **professional sociology**, in which sociological research and theory is published in journal articles that are written with other sociologists as the intended audience. Journal articles often use technical language that cannot be easily understood by people outside a particular discipline; they are accessible primarily through university libraries. As a result of limited accessibility, public sociologists critique professional sociology for having only limited impact on social activism and politics. In contrast, public sociology is composed in a way that is accessible to nonacademics. It can include books, magazines, websites, cartoons, and other forms of popular media. The goal of public sociology is to encourage public discussion of sociological issues and encourage democratic participation in social and political change.

THEORY AND PUBLIC POLICY

Sociological theories are also used to inform, evaluate, and transform **public policy**, laws and government-funded programs related to social issues. Sociological theories have enhanced our understanding of a variety of topics that garner attention from federal, state, and local governments, including poverty, housing, crime, and social inequalities, to name a few. This understanding is used to identify policy needs, evaluate the effectiveness of current policies, and assess public opinion regarding policy issues.

Sociological theory and research is used to identify characteristics of a social issue, such as how many people are affected by a particular phenomenon, and how the issue is distributed across a population. For example, to create a policy or program to help alleviate homelessness, general information about homelessness is needed. Sociologists can work with policy makers to estimate the number of people who are homeless and the causes of homelessness in a particular area. Sociological theory comes into play when making decisions about who counts as "homeless" and who does not. For example, how long does an individual or family need to be without housing to be considered homeless? Are individuals or families considered "housed" if they are temporarily staying with relatives or renting a hotel by the week? In seeking answers to questions of this kind, sociological theory helps define the concepts needed to inform public policy.

In assessing public policy needs, social theory is also an important vehicle for understanding relationships between different issues. To resolve homelessness, policy makers must attend to broader structural forces that cause homelessness, such as economic downturn, unemployment, gender inequality, domestic violence, unequal educational and job-training opportunities, and divorce. Thus, building low-income housing or temporary shelters is not likely to resolve homelessness. Addressing the social issues that contributed to or caused the homelessness is far more critical, and social theory can help policy makers see the interconnections between social issues and thus make more effective policies. These same ideas can be used to analyze the effectiveness of current public policies and provide recommendations for improvement.

Another important task for sociology is to gauge public opinion about a particular topic to assess whether a policy change will garner public support or opposition. In analyzing public opinion, sociologists uncover myths people hold as true about particular topics and assess trends in attitudes over time. For example, sociologists note that U.S. citizens are more likely to say they believe immigrants are a burden to the U.S. economy in times of economic downturn and an asset to the economy in times of economic stability. These broader public opinions also coincide with trends in laws and other public policies; when the U.S. economy is stable, immigration policies are more lenient; during times of economic downturn policies are more stringent. Sociological theory is useful in explaining the causes and consequences of these trends and predicting the likelihood of creating or revising public policy.

Summary

Sociological theory is important not only for helping sociologists understand society but for informing research practices, political activism, and public policy. In these ways, sociological theory seeks not only to understand society but to improve it. Social theory and society engage in reciprocal change, since new social conditions result in the production of new theories. These theories inform research, activism, and policy, which result in further social change. As social changes continue in the realms of technology, communications, economics, and personal and group relations, we look forward to observing the emergence of new theories and their continuing impact on our ever-changing society.

Further Reading

Denzin, Norman K., and Yvonna S. Lincoln. *The Sage Handbook of Qualitative Research,* 3rd ed. Thousand Oaks, Calif.: Sage, 2005.

Gubrium, Jaber F., and James A. Holstein. *The New Language of Qualitative Method.* New York: Oxford University Press, 1997.

Nichols, Lawrence T. *Public Sociology: The Contemporary Debate.* New Brunswick, N.J.: Transaction Publishers, 2007.

Reinharz, Shulamit. *Feminist Methods in Social Research.* New York: Oxford University Press, 1992.

GLOSSARY

adaptation   a system is able to extract from its existing environment to meet its needs

agency   individual power and free will

alienation   separation of humans from their essence

androcentric culture   collective consciousness that reflects masculine ways of understanding the world

anomaly   condition in which a society's morals and manners are incongruent

anomie   state of normlessness that occurs when there is a disjunction between societal goals and the structural ability for all individuals to achieve them

antecedent social facts   social causes of the social fact being studied

authority   power over others

both/and perspective   thought system in which cases can simultaneously belong to two or more categories

bourgeoisie   small class of wealthy owners in a capitalist society

breaching experiments   researcher breaks a social norm to observe others' reactions

capital   money put into circulation to obtain more money

capitalism   economic system based on a free market and accumulation of wealth

charismatic authority   authority derived from a likeable personality

Chicago School   theorists associated with the University of Chicago

class   group of people who share common economic standing

class consciousness   recognition of common interests among individuals with similar economic standing

C-M-C exchange   consumption; commodity-money-commodity exchange that occurs in a capitalist economy

coercion   compliance through force, often military or police

colonialism   political domination of one nation by another

color-blind racism   cultural ideology based on the belief that race is no longer significant in U.S. society and therefore opposes social policies and programs designed to alleviate racial inequality

commodity   product of labor that is given value

communicative action   social interactions among two or more people through which mutual understanding is achieved

communism   classless system in which means of production are collectively owned

conflict theory   a theory that views society as a set of unequal groups in conflict over power, resources, and values

constructivism   belief that social characteristic (sexual orientation) is strictly a social construction

critical theory   theory that analyzes the role of a society's knowledge in perpetuating inequality

cultural capital   knowledge that is highly valued in a society

cultural relativism   a way of observing and evaluating societies through the lens of their own culture rather than the lens of another culture

deviance   an act considered unacceptable by the collective

dialectical materialism   idea that societies develop through conflict

dialectic mode of logic   idea that societal knowledge progresses through conflict

discourse   formal discussions and writings about a topic

discursive formation   process of creating new concepts through discourse

docile body   object that can be used and shaped by those in positions of authority

dominant group   group that holds power in a system of domination

domination   systematic control of one group by another

double consciousness   state of internal conflict with being black and American characterized by a sense of two-ness

double hermeneutic   process of understanding something that in turn influences the thing or the people who are trying to understand

dramaturgy   symbolic interactionist theory that views social life as a series of performances

duality of structure   theory that neither agents nor structure can exist independently but are joined together in constant interaction

economic dependence   condition in which economic compensation is based not on the work individuals do but on the will and ability of another

economic independence   condition in which economic compensation is equivalent to the work performed

either/or dichotomy   thought system in which all cases naturally fit into one of two categories

emancipatory sociology   theory for the purpose of eliminating domination

empirical   something that can be verified through senses (sight, sound, touch, taste, smell)

empiricism   knowledge gained through empirical research; a set of procedures from which the findings can be verified

Enlightenment   shift in dominant mode of thought from emphasis on religion and theology to reason, rationality, and science

episteme   unconscious, collective set of accepted knowledge and beliefs that define social behavior of a given time

equilibrium   state in which opposing forces balance each other and stability is attained

essentialism   belief that a social characteristic (sexual orientation) is an indispensible part of a person's identity

ethnographic research   form of social research in which the researcher observes people in their natural surroundings to better understand their daily routines, interpersonal interactions, and other elements of social life

ethnomethodology   theory that views the social world as emerging through individuals' actions and interactions

everyday racism   uncivil treatment of an individual of one race by an individual of another race in face-to-face interactions

excessive sex distinction   exaggerated gender differences between men and women

exchange-value   value of an object based on the amount of money it can be sold for

exploitation   situation in which a person, system, or group unfairly takes advantage of another person, system, or group for personal gain

fetishism of commodities humans relating to each other through commodities as if the objects have intrinsic value while overlooking their own role in creating the objects and the meanings attributed to them

fields structured social environments in which agents use their habitus and capital to change or maintain their social positions

Frankfurt School Institute for Social Research at the University of Frankfurt

gender social and cultural expectations associated with being male or female

goal attainment when a system decides on specific goals and provides universal definitions

growth machine unfettered economic development

habitus individual's set of perceptions, dispositions, and tastes that derive from subjective experiences based on objective conditions

hegemony ideological control that creates a situation in which people willingly submit to practices that benefit the ruling class and hurt themselves because they are manipulated to misunderstand their situations

hermeneutics process of understanding something

heteronormative dominant ideology that asserts all people fall into distinct categories (male or female) and that heterosexuality is normal

Human Exemptionalist Paradigm (HEP) worldview that holds humans are separate from and above nature, and therefore exempt from consequences of misusing the environment

I subjective part of the self that acts without reflecting

ideal type prototype of some phenomenon

ideology set of beliefs and understandings about the world that systematically misrepresent, and therefore justify, the economic system in place

imperialism set of ideas and beliefs that support colonialism

indigenous people who lived in the American and African continents before European colonization

Industrial Revolution period of transformation from agriculture-based to industrial-based society

Information Revolution transformation from industrial to information-based economy

institutional racism systematic unequal treatment built into the fabric of society

integration function that oversees and directs the achievements and relationships between the other three functions of social action (A, G, & L)

interpretive sociology   methodological approach that focuses on uncovering what things mean to people and how they interpret different aspects of social life

intersubjectivity   condition in which more than one individual shares a common perception of reality

iron cage   trap of materialism humans find themselves in under a capitalistic system

laissez-faire racism   belief that racial inequality results from a lack of work ethic among blacks

language   system of symbols that facilitates communication among people in society

latency   function that allows a system to continue existing when people are not actively maintaining it

latent functions   unintended outcomes

latent interests   interests individuals are unaware of

law of the three stages   idea that all societies move through the same three stages in their development   theological, metaphysical, and positivistic

legitimation   process through which authority figures earn the right to have certain types of authority

legitimation crisis   situation in which individuals do not feel sufficiently motivated to participate in politics

life-world   the world individuals sense exists

life-world structures   parts of the life-world people use to make sense of their experiences and interactions

looking-glass self   self-perceptions developed by imagining others' perceptions

macro level   broad, overarching structures in society

majoritorian stories   truth claims generated by those with race privilege

manifest functions   obvious and intended outcomes

manifest interests   interests individuals are aware of and actively working for

manners   patterns of actions and interactions in a society

material social facts   tangible, observable social facts

matrix of domination   system of overlapping, intersecting inequalities based on individuals' configurations of race, class, and gender, which produce distinct social locations that affect experiences, privileges, and oppression individuals experience

M-C-M exchange production, or the money-commodity-money exchange that occurs in a capitalist economy

me objective part of the self that engages in self-reflection

means of production land, buildings, machines, and materials used to produce goods

mechanical solidarity social cohesion derived from shared characteristics

metanarrative broad, commonly accepted account of human historical experiences or knowledge

morals collective ideas about appropriate or inappropriate social behaviors

naturalism qualitative methodology that seeks to understand participants' interpretations of their lived experiences

New Ecological Paradigm (NEP) worldview holding that humans exist within nature, relying on and influencing their environment

nonmaterial social facts invisible social facts

normal behavior or social fact that effectively contributes to the proper functioning of society

norms standard patterns of behavior that are considered normal in a society

objectivity state of neutrality; lack of personal judgment of the researcher

old-fashioned racism belief that whites are biologically superior to blacks

organic solidarity social cohesion derived from differences, individuality, and interdependence of a society's members

paradigm broad set of ideas; general conception about how things work

party group that organizes in pursuit of power

pathological behavior or social fact that impedes the proper functioning of society

patriarchy male domination over women

patrilineage a system in which property is passed down through men, and women become the property of men

phenomenology theory that views society as mediated through individual consciousness

political activism organized actions that seek to create social change

positive science systematic way of studying something that uncovers universal laws

positivism approach that seeks to uncover verifiable laws of the social and physical world

postcolonialism interdisciplinary body of social theory that is critical of colonial rule

postmodern condition   social transformation characterized by expansion of a global market, decline in production of material goods, and an ideology that questions the validity of science

postmodern theory   theory that argues Western societies have transitioned into a postmodern era, characterized by blurred boundaries, increasing importance of media, and hypertechnology

poststructuralism   theory that analyzes language as a mechanism of power

praxis   theory designed for the purpose of social change

professional sociology   the practice of publishing sociological research and theory in journal articles written with other sociologists as the intended audience

proletariat   large class of poor workers in a capitalist society

public policy   laws and government-funded programs regarding social issues

public sociology   sociological work created for a general audience

qualitative research methods   research approach that seeks to obtain in-depth data that focuses on meanings and interpretations that guide social life

quantitative research methods   research approach that uses numbers and statistics

queer theory   branch of emancipatory theory that explores social and political definitions of gender and sexuality

rationality   use of careful calculation to determine the most efficient or effective way of completing a task

rational-legal authority   authority derived from following an established and approved procedure

rationalization   process by which people's activities become more calculated, methodical, and efficient

reflexivity   process of reflecting upon and acknowledging the personal impact researchers have on their research

reification   process by which a view of things as separate from the individuals who create them is applied to parts of society other than commodities, such as politics, government, and media

relativity   idea that meaning or value is established in relation to something else and will change according to circumstance or social group

repressive hypothesis   belief that many societies have sought to repress natural human sex drives

second shift   housework and childcare performed by women after working a full day in the paid labor sphere

sex   biological classification of being male or female, based on chromosomes, hormones, and genitalia

sexuo-economic relation   situation in which the relationship between the sexes (men and women) is an economic relationship

sign value   meaning of an object in relation to other objects of a similar type

simulacra   situation in which all objects and behaviors are imitations of real counterparts

simulation   total imitation of reality

social capital   networking and the people one knows

social constructionism   qualitative methodology that views the world as socially constructed through individuals' interactions and analyzes how people construct their social lives

social distribution of knowledge   way in which knowledge is divided among society's members

social dynamics   study of social change that focuses on patterns in how societies change over time

social facts   things that are generalizable, or occur in the same way in all similar societies

social function   contribution of a particular social structure to the operation and stability of society as a whole

social institutions (also referred to as institutions)   broad social structures in society that have a recognized purpose

social solidarity   ways in which societies are held together

social statics   study that focuses on the parts of society and their relationships to each other and the larger social system

social stock of knowledge   set of facts and ideas that exist and can be known in a society or social group

social stratification   ranking of society's members in a hierarchy

social structure   part of society that is separate from the individuals within the society, but that guides their actions in patterned ways

social theory   set of ideas about how society works

socialism   system in which the government owns and operates the major institutions in society such as education and healthcare

society   system of patterned interactions that encompasses a social structure, social institutions and social interactions in everyday life

sociolinguistics   academic discipline that analyzes the role of language in societies

sociological determinism   idea that individuals' actions directly result from external forces and social structures rather than individual agency

status   prestige or honor recognized by others

structural functionalism   theory that focuses on broad social structures and institutions in society

structuralism   theory that analyzes the impact of language on human thoughts

structuration   theory that argues a two-way relationship exists between structure and individual action

subjective   an individual's personal interpretations, experiences or opinions rather than an outside perspective or evidence

subordinate group   group that lacks power in a system of domination

subsystem   structure or part within a larger system

suffrage   right to vote

survival of the fittest   the evolutionary idea that individuals with the most desirable traits will be selected for reproduction, thereby passing along those traits to future generations within the species

symbol   something that represents something else

symbolic capital   honor, prestige, or status

symbolic interactionism   theory that views society as individuals interacting in everyday life

symbolic racism   combination of negative feelings toward blacks and the belief that blacks violate core American values that cause continuing racial inequality

symbolic value   meaning a person or society gives an object; what an object symbolizes about the person who owns it

synthesis   a process in which conflicting elements of multiple theories are combined into a new, unified theory

system   complex whole formed from related parts

theory   set of ideas about how something works

traditional authority   authority derived from customs or habits

treadmill of consumption   continual consumption of material goods; (C-M-C)

treadmill of production   continual production of material goods; (M-C-M)

urbanization   growth of cities

use value   value of an object based on its practical application

validity   agreed upon logic or correctness of something

value-free sociology   research approach in which sociologists set their own values and opinions aside and approach research topics from a neutral position

veil   something that blocks individuals from seeing another person's true self

white privilege   advantages granted to all whites, knowingly or unknowingly, from the system of racism in U.S. society

world economy   situation in which a group of nations maintain economic control over others

world empire   situation in which one or a few countries take political control over others, usually through military conquest.

BIBLIOGRAPHY

Best, Steven, and Douglas Kellner. *Postmodern Theory: Critical Interrogations.* New York: The Guilford Press, 1991.

Calhoun, Craig. *Critical Social Theory.* Malden, Mass.: Blackwell Publishers, 1995.

Cuff, E.C., W.W. Sharrock, and D.W. Francis. *Perspectives in Sociology*, 5th ed. London: Routledge, 2006.

Holstein, James A., and Jaber F. Gubrium. *Inner Lives and Social Worlds: Readings in Social Psychology.* New York: Oxford University Press, 2003.

Lengermann, Patricia Madoo, and Jill Niebrugge-Brantley. *The Women Founders: Sociology and Social Theory, 1830–1930.* New York: McGraw-Hill, 1998.

Lorber, Judith. *Gender Inequality: Feminist Theories and Politics*, 2nd ed. Los Angeles: Roxbury Publishing Company, 2001.

Ritzer, George. *Sociological Theory*, 8th ed. New York: McGraw-Hill, 2011.

Ritzer, George. *Classical Sociological Theory*, 5th ed. New York: McGraw-Hill, 2008.

Turner, Jonathan H. *The Structure of Sociological Theory*, 7th ed. Belmont, Calif.: Wadsworth, 2003.

Turner, Jonathan H., Leonard Beeghley, and Charles H. Powers. *The Emergence of Sociological Theory*, 6th ed. Belmont, Calif.: Thomson Wadsworth, 2007.

INDEX

A

action system 58–60
adaptation 58
Adorno, Theodor 15, 81, 83, 84
agency 68–70, 78, 99
alienation 30–31
androcentric culture 46–47
anomaly 25–28
anomie 61
antecedent social facts 8–9
authority 50–51, 62

B

Baudrillard, Jean 16–17, 96–99
Blumer, Herbert 15, 66, 68–70, 119–120, 136
both/and perspective 114
Bourdieu, Pierre 17, 100–102
bourgeoisie 31–33, 53, 65
breaching experiments 78–79

C

capital 30, 101
capitalism 9, 12, 14, 28–33, 49–50, 53, 64–65,
    81–84, 107–108, 109–110, 129–130
charismatic authority 51

Chicago School 15, 57, 65–66, 68, 138
class 17, 31–33, 51, 106, 113–115
class consciousness 32
C-M-C exchange 30, 130–132
coercion 84
colonialism 106, 113, 116, 124–125 (*see also*
    colonization, postcolonialism)
colonization 115–117
color–blind racism 121–122
commodity 17, 30, 81–84, 95
communism 29, 32–33
Comte, Auguste 8–9, 12, 19–24, 37
conflict 28, 31–33, 42, 47, 62–65
conflict theory 14–15, 62–65, 72, 81, 86, 102
constructivism 127–128
Cooley, Charles Horton 15, 66, 68
Cooper, Anna Julia 13, 17, 39–42, 54
critical race theory 122–124
critical theory 15, 73, 81–86
    Gramsci 81
    Habermas 81
    Lukacs 81–84
    Marx and 15, 81–82
    Weber and 15, 81
cultural capital 101
cultural relativism 25–26

D

Dahrendorf, Ralf 14, 62–64
deviance 61, 72
dialectical materialism 28, 32
dialectic mode of logic 28
discourse 26, 90–92
discursive formation 90–92, 94, 126–127
division of labor 22, 31, 36, 110–111
 household 110–111
docile body 92–94
dominant group 39, 42, 62, 109–110, 114,
 119–120, 133, 137, 140
 gender 109–110
 group positioning theory 119–120
 race 39, 119–120
domination 16, 24–27, 39, 115–116
 colonization and 115–116
 critical theory and 84
 gender 27
 and language 16, 115–116
 race 26–27, 39
 and science 81, 85–86
double consciousness 52–53
double hermeneutic 100
dramaturgy 66, 70–71
Du Bois, W. E. B. 13–14, 17, 51–54, 138
Durkheim, Emile 7–9, 12, 14, 19, 33–37,
 57–58, 78–79, 81, 108, 138
duality of structure 99–100

E

eco-feminism 132–133
economic dependence 45–46
economic independence 44–46
either/or dichotomy 113–114
emancipatory sociology 17, 105–133, 137
 environmental theories 130–133
 feminist theories 105–117
 theories of nonhuman animals 17,
  129–130
 postcolonialism 124–125
 queer theory 125–129
 theories of race and ethnicity 119–124
empirical 20–21, 23, 85
empiricism 21, 23
Engels, Frederick 29, 109–110
Enlightenment 11–13, 81
environmental theories 130–133

episteme 89–90
equilibrium 42, 57, 60–62
essentialism 127–128
ethnographic research 77, 136
ethnomethodology 15, 73, 77–80, 86, 137
everyday racism 41
excessive sex distinction 45–46
exchange value 30, 97, 132
exploitation 31, 65, 109–111, 119–120,
 129–130 (*see also* exploitive labor)
 capitalism and 31
 class 31
 gender 109–111
 global 65
 nonhuman animals 129–130
 race 119–120
exploitive labor 109–111

F

family 22, 27, 47
feminist theories 17, 105–117, 130, 132
 (*see also* women's movement)
 eco-feminism 132–133
 indigenous feminism 106, 115–117
 intersectional feminism 106, 113–115
 liberal feminism 106–108
 Marxist feminism 106, 109–111
 and theories of nonhuman animals 130
 radical feminism 106, 112–113
 womanism 106, 115
fetishism of commodities 81–84
Feudal Era 14
fields 101–102
Foucault, Michel 16, 89–94, 125–127
Frankfurt School 15, 81, 83, 84, 85

G

Garfinkel, Harold 15, 77–79
gender 45–46, 79–80, 108 (see also feminist
 theories, gender inequality)
gender inequality 43–47, 108, 110, 113, 117,
 139
Giddens, Anthony 17, 99–100, 102
Gilman, Charlotte Perkins 12, 17, 43–47, 54
goal attainment 58
Goffman, Erving 66, 70–72
Gramsci, Antonio 15, 81, 84

group positioning theory 119–120
growth machine 132

H

Habermas, Jurgen 15, 81, 85–86
habitus 100–102
hegemony 84
hermeneutics 100
heteronormative 125–127
Human Exemptionalist Paradigm 132–133
Husserl, Edmund 15, 73–74, 85

I

I 66
ideal type 47–49
ideology 32, 41, 46, 121–122, 125
imperialism 124
indigenous 116
indigenous feminism 106, 113, 115–117
Industrial Revolution 11–12, 36, 47, 109–110
Information Revolution 17
institutional racism 41
institutions 4, 33
integration 58, 60
interpretive sociology 25
intersectional feminism 106, 113–115
intersubjectivity 76–77
iron cage 50, 81

K

knowledge 17, 73–77, 89–96, 100–102,
    123–125
        as commodity 95–96
        and colonialism 124–125
        and domination 85–86
        intersubjective 76–77
        objective 17, 100–102
        and power 95–96
        and racism 123–124
        and social control 89–94
        subjective 17, 73–76, 94–95, 100–102

L

laissez–faire racism 120–121
language 8, 16, 22, 79, 89, 99, 102, 116, 129
latency 58, 60

latent functions 61
law of the three stages 22–23
legitimation 96
legitimation crisis 85–86
liberal feminism 106–108, 110, 114–115
life-world 73–76, 136
life-world structures 75–76
looking-glass self 66, 68
Lukacs, Georgy 81–84
Lyotard, Jean-Francois 16–17, 95–96

M

macro level 60
majoritorian stories 123–124
manifest functions 61
manifest interests 63
manners 24–28, 41
Martineau, Harriet 12–13, 23–28, 37
Marx, Karl 12, 14, 15, 17, 19, 28–33, 37, 53, 57,
    62, 65, 81–82, 97, 109–111, 129–132, 138
        conflict theory 14, 57, 62
        critical theory and 15, 81
        emancipatory sociology and 17, 105
        environmental theories and 130–132
        and feminism 105, 109–111
        postmodern theory and 97
        theories of nonhuman animals and
            129–130
Marxist feminism 106, 109–111
material social facts 34
matrix of domination 113–115
M-C-M exchange 30, 50, 130–132
me 66
Mead, George Herbert 15, 66–68
means of production 28, 32, 130
mechanical solidarity 35–36
media 17, 83–84, 95–99
Merton, Robert 14, 60–61
metanarrative 95–96
Modern Era 14, 16, 89, 92
morals 24–28

N

New Ecological Paradigm 132
nonmaterial social facts 34
normal 34–35
norms 25, 33, 57–58, 60–61, 68, 78–79

O

objectivity 100, 113, 135–136
old-fashioned racism 120–121
organic solidarity 35–36

P

Parsons, Talcott 14, 58–61
Paradigm 57, 72–73, 89, 99, 103
party 50–51
pathological 21, 34–35, 94
patriarchy 105–106, 112–113, 116
patrilineage 109
phenomenology 15, 73–77, 86
political activism 135, 137–140
positive science 8, 12, 20
positivism 20, 23, 135
postcolonialism 17, 105, 119, 124–125, 133
postmodern condition 16–17
postmodern theory 16–17, 89, 94–99
poststructuralism 16, 89–94, 102
power 16–17, 27, 62, 64–65, 81, 84–86, 99,
    112–115, 124–125
        colonialism and 124–125
        gender and 112–113
        and knowledge 16, 85–86
        and language 16
        matrix of domination and 113–115
        and sociology 17
pragmatism 65–66
praxis 105, 122, 137–138
production 12, 28–31, 47, 50, 109–111, 130–132
professional sociology 138
proletariat 31–33, 65, 81
public policy 139–140
public sociology 138–139

Q

qualitative research methods 15, 25–26, 135–137
quantitative research methods 9, 25, 33, 36,
    135–137
queer theory 17, 105, 119, 125–129, 133

R

race 17, 26–27, 51–54, 61, 113–115, 119–124
    (*see also* theories of race and ethnicity)
theories of race and ethnicity 17, 105,
    119–124
        color-blind racism 121–122

critical race theory 122–124
group positioning theory 119–120
symbolic racism 120–122
racism 13, 17, 40–42, 51, 53, 61, 106–107,
    113–115, 119–123
        color-blind 121–122
        everyday 41
        feminist theories and 106
        institutional 41, 51
        and knowledge 41, 123–124
        laissez-faire 120–121
        matrix of domination and 113–115
        old-fashioned 120–121
        in sociology 13, 17
        symbolic 120–122
        women's rights and 40–41, 106–107
radical feminism 106, 112–113
rationality 11–12, 14
rational-legal authority 51
rationalization 47, 51, 81
reflexivity 113
reification 81–84
relativity 136
religion 11–14, 22, 46, 49–50, 54, 132
repressive hypothesis 94
research methods 9, 15, 20–21, 23, 25–26 36,
    77, 79–80, 112–113, 135–137, 140
        conversation analysis 79–80
        ethnography 77, 136
        ethnomethodology 137
        experimentation 21
        feminist 112–113, 140
        historical research 21
        naturalism 136
        objectivity 113, 135
        positivism 20, 135
        qualitative 15, 25–26, 135–137
        quantitative 9, 36, 135–137
        scientific 136–137, 140
        social constructionism 137

S

Schutz, Alfred 15, 73–77
science 8–9, 11–12, 14–15, 17, 23–25, 81,
    85–86, 136–137, 140
        critical theory and 15, 81, 85–86
        critical science 23–25
        and domination 81, 85–86
        Durkheim and 8–9

emancipatory sociology critique of 137
feminist critique of 140
Martineau and 23–24
phenomenology critique of 136
postmodern theory and 17, 89, 95–96
sociology as 8–9, 23–24
symbolic interactionist critique of 136
Weber and 9, 47–49
second shift 110–111
self 53, 66–68, 70–72, 102
sex 108
sexism 13, 106–117 (see also patriarchy)
feminist theories and 106–117
in sociology 13
sexuality 27, 94, 112–113, 125–130
queer theory and 125–129
radical feminism and 112
sexuo-economic relation 43–46
sign value 98–99
simulacra 97–99
simulation 97–99
social capital 101
social distribution of knowledge 74
social dynamics 22–23
social facts 8–9, 33–35, 78
social function 33–34
social institutions 4, 6–7, 15, 32, 53, 84, 89,
    99, 122
social solidarity 35–36, 54, 62
social statics 22
social stock of knowledge 74
social stratification 50–51
social structure 4–7, 15, 17, 22, 33, 58, 64,
    68–70, 78–79, 99
social theory 3–9, 15, 122, 124, 135, 138–140
society 6–8
sociolinguistics 16
sociological determinism 68–70
sociology 6, 8–9, 11–18, 20–21, 23–25, 47–49,
    112–113
    definitions of 6, 8–9, 20–21, 23–25,
        47–49
    history of 11–18
status 50
structural functionalism 4–8, 14–17, 22, 33,
    57–62, 68–70, 72, 77–79, 105
    Comte 22
    Durkheim 7, 14, 33
    Merton 60–61
    Parsons 58–60

structuralism 16
structuration 17, 99
subaltern studies 125
subjective 15, 17, 66, 73, 76–77, 86, 100–101, 136
subordinate group 17, 39, 42, 62, 109–110,
    114, 119–120, 137
    gender 109–110
    group positioning theory 119–120
    race 119–120
subsystems 60
suffrage 39, 107
survival of the fittest 43
symbol 8, 15, 96, 98–99, 129, 131
symbolic capital 101
symbolic interactionism 6–8, 14–15, 17, 57,
    65–72, 78, 86, 105, 119, 136
    Blumer 68–70, 136
    Chicago School 15, 57, 65–66
    Cooley 68
    Goffman 70–72
    Mead 66–68
symbolic racism 120–122
symbolic value 98–99
synthesis 17, 28, 32, 89, 99–103
system 58, 64

T
theory 3–9
traditional authority 51
treadmill of consumption 130–132
treadmill of production 130–132

U
urbanization 12, 14
use value 30, 97–98, 132

V
validity 76
value-free sociology 9, 48
veil 53

W
Wallerstein, Immanuel 14, 62, 64–65
Weber, Max 9, 12, 14–15, 39, 47–51, 54,
    57–58, 132, 134
    conflict theory 14, 57
    critical theory 15
    environmental theories and 134

white privilege 123
womanism 106, 115
women 26–27, 39–42, 43–47, 54, 105–117 (see also women's movement, sex, gender)
women's movement 39–42, 105–107 (see also feminist theories)
world economy 64–65
world empire 64